A BOOK *for* EVERY WOMAN

Published by the National Library of Australia
Canberra ACT 2600

© National Library of Australia 2010

Books published by the National Library of Australia further the Library's objectives to interpret and highlight the Library's collections and to support the creative work of the nation's writers and researchers.

Every reasonable endeavour has been made to contact the copyright holders. Where this has not been possible, the copyright holders are invited to contact the publisher.

This book is copyright in all countries subscribing to the Berne Convention. Apart from any fair dealing for the purpose of research, criticism or review, as permitted under the *Copyright Act 1968*, no part may be reproduced by any process without written permission. Enquiries should be made to the publisher.

National Library of Australia Cataloguing-in-Publication entry

Title:	A book for every woman/Associated School of Dressmaking Sydney (National Library of Australia)
ISBN:	9780642277107 (hbk)
Subjects:	Home economics—Australia.
	Women—Health and hygiene—Australia.
	Beauty, Personal—Australia.
Other Authors/Contributors:	
	National Library of Australia.
	Associated School of Dressmaking (Sydney).
Dewey Number:	640.994

Publication manager: Susan Hall

Designer: Elizabeth Faul

Additional text: Michelle Mortimer

Additional picture research: Felicity Harmey

Printer: Imago Australia Pty Ltd

A note on the original text

As the twentieth century progressed, the role of the Australian housewife became firmly established. No longer the Victorian mistress of the home, with servants at her command, the housewife of the early 1900s had to be a skilled cleaner, seamstress, cook and home economist, whilst maintaining her feminine grace in conversation, demeanour and appearance. The popular tradition of women's household advice literature in the late nineteenth century continued to flourish into the 1920s and 1930s. Newspapers published columns recommending cleaning products to use; women's magazines, like the *Everylady's Journal*, discussed issues ranging from dining etiquette and beauty hints to laundry and cooking tips; and handbooks covered every practical aspect of domestic activity. *A Book for Every Woman* was one such book. It was published in 1924 by the Sydney-based Associated School of Dressmaking, established in 1918 to provide women with lessons in dressmaking and millinery 'by post'. Subscribers could learn to make their own clothes at home following the easy-to-follow instruction manuals, saving money on their wardrobe without neglecting the latest fashion trends. The advice found in the pages of *A Book for Every Woman* conveys the same ethos of domestic self-improvement promoted by the Associated School. It claims to provide readers with 'much that is wise, a great deal inspirational and everything practical ... in relation to cooking and household hints ... and all matters of health, beauty and conduct'. Whether the housewife seeks general advice on 'How To Make Baby Happy', 'How To Be Graceful', or the ideal measurements of the perfect feminine figure, *A Book for Every Woman* really does contain something for every woman.

This reproduction has been augmented with illustrations from Myer Emporium catalogues and other advertising pamphlets of the time, all held by the National Library of Australia. Full captions appear on pages 186–187.

A BOOK for EVERY WOMAN

1924

First Edition

Price
5/-

Published by
ASSOCIATED SCHOOL
OF DRESSMAKING
SYDNEY, N.S.W.

Foreword

EVERY woman will find in this book much that is wise, a great deal inspiring and everything practical.

¶ The object in compiling it has been to publish only that which has been tested and proved, not only in relation to cooking and household hints, but also on all matters of health, beauty and conduct.

¶ The young mother will find helpful hints relating to the care of infants and the management of children, she who is desirous of making her own garments will find many pages of interesting information, the girl or woman who is interested in retaining youth and a good appearance will discover a wealth of desirable knowledge, in fact, for every girl and woman this book will prove of incalculable value and convenience.

¶ Develop the habit of consulting its pages regularly, and you will be repaid a hundredfold.

Rosalie Blythe
Editress.

Two Walks

Last week I walked a certain street,
    And met such gloomy folk;
I made great haste to pass them by,
    And neither smiled nor spoke.

The giant elms drooped sullenly,
    The very sun was dim;
I met a friend and said: "I hope
    I've seen the last of him!"

To-day I walked that very street
    And loved the folks I met;
If business had not made me leave,
    I would be talking yet.

Of course you've solved the mystery—
    'Tis very plain to see;
The day I met the gloomy folks,
    The gloom was inside me!
                —Sheila O'Neill.

Our own feelings make all the difference in the world in the way things look to us; most of us have proved this to be true over and over again, haven't we?

When we are happy, when we are seeing the bright side, the sun shines and the birds sing, there is no gloom anywhere, and people are so friendly and good-natured that it is very easy to think the best of them. Doesn't it behove us, then, when we find ourselves peering through blue glasses, to change our own mental attitude? Surely it does; and this isn't at all a difficult thing to do, once we set about it cheerily and determinedly.

The first thing is to know it is what we desire, above most other things, to do, then to declare for its accomplishment; and we may well accept as a bit of encouragement the fact that every effort in the right direction makes the next easier. Suppose we awake in the morning with a feeling that everything is going wrong—that the world is hollow and our particular doll is stuffed with sawdust!

A little self-analysis will show us that there is no real reason for this; affairs were bright enough yesterday, and nothing has changed but our viewpoint. The sane and sensible thing to do, then, is to give it yet another shift, and bring back the happier outlook. Begin at once to think of pleasant things, and look for them, and speak of them. Mention the fact at breakfast that the tea is delicious, and the toast browned to a turn. Make merry over some little innocent joke. Resolutely keep on the sunny side until you find you are really there.

More easily said than done? Yet it is easily done, and the reward is great. We know there are troubles—real sorrows—which strike deep; we know that from these not one of us is exempt. But to be gloomy does not help us to bear them more bravely, does not assuage them in the least for ourselves or others, rather the contrary. It is well for all, here and beyond, that we steadfastly "look to the light."

M. Coue, the little "apostle" of self-healing, applies these teachings in a remarkable degree. His formula or slogan, "Ce passe," relates to mental as well as physical ills; hence we may declare "It is going away, it is going, it is going, it is going, going—gone!" of a heartache, or intense depression of spirits, as well as of bodily pain. And with equal assurance of success.

M. Coue's own method or practise is as follows: "If you are suffering from any severe pain, such as toothache or headache, sit down, close your eyes and assure yourself that you are going to get rid of it. Now gently stroke with your hand the affected part, and repeat at the same as fast as you can, producing a continuous stream of sound, the words 'It's going, going, going—gone!' Keep it up for about a minute, pausing only to take a deep breath, when necessary, and using the word 'gone' only at conclusion of the whole proceeding.

At the end of this time the pain will either have entirely ceased or at least sensibly abated. If the pain has ceased, suggest that it will not return; if it has only diminished, suggest that it will shortly pass away altogether. Now return to whatever employment you were engaged in; let other interests occupy your attention. It is no exaggeration to say that by this process any pain can be conquered.

It may be, in extreme cases, that you will have to return several times to the attack. But do not be discouraged; attack it firmly and you are bound to succeed.

The same procedure is equally effective with distressing states of worry, fear, despondency. In such cases the stroking movement should be applied to the forehead.

For years M. Coue has thought and studied along these lines, earnestly and without recompense save the hope of benefiting his fellows; and from the experiments which he has made daily for nearly a quarter century, he has reached the conclusion, among others, that "every illness, whatever it may be, can yield to auto-suggestion, daring and unlikely as the statement may seem; I do not say it does always yield, but can yield."

All our lives we have been using this power—unconsciously mainly, and in a determined way. Every time we say, "I am sick," or wretched, or unhappy, or that any unpleasant condition belongs to us, every time we harbor a definite fear, we are sowing the seed for a harvest most undesirable, to say the least; we are giving an auto-suggestion for what we do not wish, and when we get what we have bargained for, we wonder why such trials are visited upon us.

The answer is that we, like little children, are learning, and can only learn in the school of experience. From his own experience M. Coue has deduced the fact that the subconscious mind can be reached and consciously influenced to right action by the repetition of a phrase audibly—by saying the same thing over and over in a whisper so distinct that the ear can catch it, if not aloud, or at least moving the lips; hence his famous formula or slogan: "Day by day in every way I am getting better and better."

His own recommendation is that this be repeated twenty times, counting mechanically on a long string with twenty knots in it, every evening as soon as you are in bed and every morning before getting up. As the words "in every way" apply to everything, you need not think of anything particular.

Any suggestion of good, present and to come, will serve as well; he provided this simple formula so that it might reach everyone—as it has surely done. And the meat in the cocoanut is here: "Make this auto-suggestion with confidence, with faith, with the certainty of obtaining what you want.

"The greater the conviction, the greater and the more rapid will be the results obtained." Use the knowledge you have, faithfully, persistently, and more will be given you. And be very sure to "let your light shine," passing on to others the good you get.

I WILL.

I will start anew this morning with a higher, fairer creed;
I will cease to stand complaining of my ruthless neighbour's greed;
I will cease to sit repining while my duty's call is clear,
I will waste no moment whining and my heart shall know no fear.
I will look sometimes about me for the things that merit praise;
I will search for hidden beauties that elude the grumbler's gaze;
I will try to find contentment in the paths that I must tread,
I will cease to have resentment when another moves ahead.
I will not be swayed by envy when my rival's strength is shown;
I will not deny his merit, but I'll strive to prove my own;
I will try to see the beauty spread before me, rain or shine—
I will cease to preach your duty and be more concerned with mine.

Do You Make Work for Yourself ?

"I don't see how you manage to look so well with all your family cares," said the worried woman to her rosy-cheeked friend. "Now looking after my little girl and keeping the house as it should be wears me all out, while you have four children and yet you never seem tired. How in the world do you manage?"

The rosy-cheeked matron laughed. "I get tired and flustered sometimes just the same as anybody else, for naturally I have a good deal to do, but I systematize it as well as I can and try to make things as easy for myself as possible, but I think the real reason I get along so well is because I never make work for myself."

"Make work, what do you mean? I never make work for myself, that's not necessary. There is enough to do without that, goodness knows."

But the rosy-cheeked woman saw that this was one of the times when truth would do far more good than politeness and said bravely, "According to my ideas you do. You are always thinking of what you can do to improve your house, of what new dresses you can afford to make for little Dorothy, or of some new kind of fancy work you can make for presents, or else you busy yourself with totally unecessary cleaning. That's what I call 'making work.' All these things are pleasant to have or to do, but they are not worth worrying or getting tired over. They are not absolutely necessary. Your house can get along well enough with a thorough cleaning every week and a little dusting and easy brushing up. Dorothy has already more clothes than are good for her, and no sensible woman should ruin her eyes by doing fancy work when she is feeling tired. Forgive me for speaking plainly, but I can't bear to see you wear yourself out as you do."

For a moment the worried little woman looked offended, but, as she knew from long experience how really kind-hearted her friend was she decided to think it over before she said anything in her own defence, and the more she thought the less she could say.

It is only by realizing what things are of real importance and what others are non-essential and by planning so as to simplify her tasks that a woman with children and household tasks to attend to can manage to get along and preserve her health and good spirits. But while I am preaching the doctrine of not "making work," do not for a minute understand me to mean that I approve of a shiftlessly run household. The woman who from laziness or lack of planning allows her home to get in this condition is not worthy of having any.

She is not simplifying her work by cutting out the non-essentials, she is, to put it in business parlance, "neglecting her job."

If you feel that you are overworked look around your house and see how you can make things easier for yourself without sacrificing the essentials of wholesome living which are, of course, cleanliness and nutritious food. Does the cleaning up after breakfast take too long a time every morning? If this is the trouble there are two remedies that suggest themselves. The first is to train the family to pick up their things and not leave them around for other people to do. Even small children can be taught to "help mother" by picking up their toys or clothing, but of course if all their little lives they have been allowed to throw things about you must not expect miracles in a day, for force of habit is very strong. It will take patience, perseverence, and even a few mild punishments by depriving them of something they like, to bring them into a more orderly state of mind. Older girls and boys or refractory husbands should have the selfishness of expecting an already over-burdened housewife to pick up after them fully and kindly explained and they will make strenuous efforts to lighten the household work in this respect. Most of such untidy habits come merely from thoughtlessness and lack of training in that great work-saver, order.

It may be, however, that you are doing a lot of unnecessary work every day because your house is over-furnished. Is the mantel loaded with ornaments, the top of the bureau filled with fripperies and the walls overloaded with pictures? Try putting away some of these things and notice how more restful your home looks and how much work this saves.

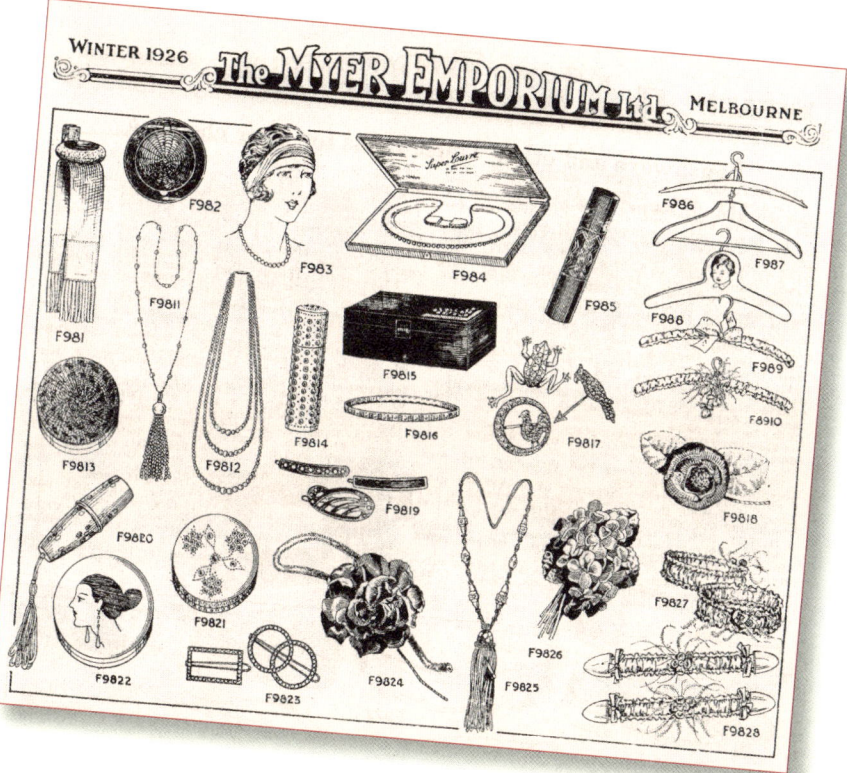

I shall never forget the length of time it used to take me to dust my bedroom every day or so. One morning when I was especially hurried I suddenly woke up to the fact that I was doing a lot of unnecessary work. First I went at my bureau which looked like a fancy table at a fair. I rubbed my eyes with astonishment before the mass of things which my little duster had patiently passed over and around so conscientiously day after day. My room was a great deal prettier without them. The things I did care for and want to have about me showed up as they could not when closely elbowed by things I did not care especially about, and there was an atmosphere of restfulness and calm in my room that it had never had. I clapped my hands when I calculated the few minutes it would take me to set it to rights in the mornings.

Then I turned my attention to the sitting-room and dining-room and even the kitchen came in for its share of this weeding out process. I found I had a cupboard full of kitchen and other household utensils that we never used because they were too big or too little, or too something or other, that made them unserviceable. For instance, there was an ice-chest that was too big for our family and a preserving kettle that was not satisfactory, etc. The things were all good in themselves so I had kept them. I sold the contents of this cupboard. The sum of money realized was not large, but it was enough to buy a new ice-chest, more suitable to the needs of our family, and several little labor-saving devices for the kitchen, which we had felt we could not afford. In short, in this cleaning-up process, I laid a firm hand upon everything, no matter how tiny, that I was saving with a view to its being of possible use some day and asked myself if it would really probably be of use and if it would pay for its storing. It was simply extraordinary how many of these things I decided would do more good given away to people who could put them into use at once. Try this weeding out process in your own home and see if it does not save work.

House Cleaning Made Easy

The old-fashioned idea of the necessity for a spring and autumn housecleaning is becoming a thing of the past in most households, for which we modern housewives should be truly grateful. By doing simple housecleaning often and the heavier work a little at a time, you save both yourself and belongings.

The first thing to consider in keeping the house clean, is to keep dirt from getting into the house by keeping walks, steps, porches and sills, together with shoes and rubbers, as clean as possible; and when the dust is removed, it should be removed thoroughly. Right methods mean the removal of dirt—not merely scattering it about to settle again. Another thing which will be of inestimable value in lightening the burdens of housecleaning, is to train the family to put things they use where they belong, and in good condition. This is only fair play to all.

Many housewives use water and cleaning agents too lavishly in cleaning woodwork and furniture. This not only injures the wood and finishes, but weakens glue, paste and cement. Many good cleaning agents are sold in boxes under trade names. These are convenient and are usually in handy-sized boxes. A pure, mild white soap is preferable to the stronger varieties containing alkali, which usually injures finishes. A little kerosene added to your cleaning water will help to cut the grease and thus free the dirt. Borax and ammonia are wonderful aids in housecleaning, to cut grease and soften the water. One tablespoon of borax or two tablespoons of ammonia to a gallon of water is sufficient.

Different kinds of scourers are suitable for different kinds of cleaning. Whiting is especially adopted to fine surfaces. It should be mixed with water for aluminium, kerosene for enameled iron and porcelain and with am-

monia for silver. Bathbrick is coarser and more suited for iron, zinc and steel. This should be applied with a little water or if the surface to be cleaned is very soiled, a little kerosene may be added. Steelwool is used for the removal of stains and discolorations from hard metal or wood surfaces. A fine grade of wool should be used for this purpose.

Your cleaning tools should be in repair and ready before the cleaning proper starts, but before buying any new equipment ask yourself a few questions. Will it make some disagreeable task more pleasant? Will it really pay for itself in the long run by wear and tear lessened or by time and strength saved?

Keep your cleaning things together in some convenient place and always put them away clean. Keep your brooms, mops and brushes hanging up when not in use. Long handles on brooms, mops and dust pans are great back-savers.

A dirty carpet sweeper is never efficient so should be cleaned frequently. The box should be emptied on to a damp newspaper and all hairs and dirt removed from the brushes with a stiff comb, using the coarse teeth.

All cleaning cloths should be soft and loosely woven so that they will take up dirt easily and be easy to clean. If a few drops of linseed oil or water are sprinkled on the duster it will take up the dust instead of merely scattering it, but care must be taken not to use too much oil or moisture, as it will leave streaks.

The walls, whether painted or papered, should never be allowed to become badly soiled or dusty, as the dust becomes ground into the walls, causing them to present a dingy appearance. They should be wiped down occasionally with a soft, long-handled brush or a broom covered with a soft flannel bag. Oil-painted walls may be washed with a cloth well wrung out of warm, light suds made with pure white soap. Glazed wall paper may be cleaned in the same way, but care must be taken not to leave any moisture as it will seep through at the seams and loosen the paper.

Mirrors and windows may be kept bright and shining with only an occasional washing if they are rubbed frequently with soft paper. Toilet paper serves this purpose admirably. When it is necessary to wash them, use a lintless cloth, well wrung out of clear, hot water, to which a little washing soda has been added. In cold weather it is often desirable to dry-clean the windows. This may be done by rubbing on a paste made by moistening a fine powder such as whiting. Spread on with a soft cloth and when dry rub off and polish with a soft cloth or paper.

All woodwork should be dusted frequently. If all spots and finger marks around door knobs, handles, window latches, etc., are cleaned frequently with a dampened cloth it will save labor and wear.

One should be careful not to use too much water, soap or cleaning powder on unfinished woodwork as it will discolor the wood. Painted woodwork should be cleaned the same as oil-painted walls, but soap should never be rubbed directly on the surface to be cleaned, as it dulls and softens the paint. Clear hot water should be used for cleaning enamel painted woodwork, as this treatment does not harm the gloss or dull the enamel as does soap. If the woodwork is oiled or varnished it should be cleaned with an oil duster or mop unless it has become dingy and black, in which case it may be washed like paint. Rubbing with a soft cloth that has been liberally sprinkled with linseed oil and furniture polish, will revive dingy varnish wonderfully. Never use any kind of oil on waxed woodwork as it softens the wax so that dirt may settle into it.

Matting may be cleaned by sweeping with a soft brush and an occasional wiping with a dampened cloth. In washing linoleum, care must be taken not to use too much water as it gets underneath and gradually rots the covering and the floor.

All furniture, as well as everything else about the house, should be dusted frequently. A soft brush is ideal for this and an oil brush or duster may be used for leather upholstered furniture.

The whole secret of easy housecleaning is to keep clean rather than make clean. Any housewife would do well to make this her housecleaning motto: "Easy and Often."

Love Your Work

When the sun tilts over the horizon line calling us from sleep, we start up with a sense that our world, just like our bedroom, must be made up anew. All the tasks we did yesterday must be repeated or carried further. Just so when the pause and listlessness of Summer pass, and Autumn's foreboding of Winter puts new tingles in the air, up and awake come our energies and out we go to our work of creation with a fresh vitality and higher hopes. That much effort Nature takes off our shoulders, that energy itself is rhythmic and periodic. It dies down at night and wakes alert and glad with the morning; it becomes drowsy and listless with Summer and laughs aloud as it shoulders its Autumnal burden.

There is no stancher friend in the world than necessary work. Work is truly what keeps alive in us our zest for living. That undone task calling to our hand—that man to be fed, that child to teach and encourage, that growing desire to put daily one more bit of the world in order and firmly established in the right way—believe me, that is what makes life worth living.

We all take up our tasks and carry them on despite weariness, in the firm belief that our children, or somebody's children will take up life on a firmer and securer basis than we did. We toil hoping that those who come after us may have a little more joy than we had and meet fewer obstacles than we fought against. It matters not whether we have children of our own or immediate claims; the next generation is really our child, and Everyman is truly our brother, and our successors must all stand higher than we because they stand on the shoulders of our untiring work.

Work requires love just as much as anything else. Love, you know, is the creative force. Out of the love of God came all creation. To this day work is only the creative act, but love is the power from which it flows. So I should like to advise all of you who will listen to me either to learn to love the work you do; or, if you can not, stop and take up a work you can love.

There is an opinion altogether too broadcast that some work is delightful and lovable and some work not so. A certain great philosopher tells an amusing tale of himself. As he sat in his study working he looked out of the window and saw a man breaking up stones in the pavement. Hour after hour, as the philosopher set down words on the paper, the man outside in the street continued to ply his pick. The philosopher felt so sorry for the man that finally he could stand it no longer and he hastened out to him and accosted him. "What do you think of all day as you keep on hour after hour breaking stones?" The man stood up, rested his pick against his hip, spat on his hands and rubbed them together with a broad grin and replied: "Breakin' stones," and lifted his pick again. The philosopher withdrew to his study a happier and a wiser man, knowing that each man gravitates naturally to the work he enjoys thinking about.

Roads must be made, and it is better to be a cheerful and eager road-maker, than a fretful or listless artist. If your work chances to be cleaning and tidying up a home, weeding and planting and watering a garden or sewing on garments to be worn, or handling some part of a great machine in a big factory, you must learn to love it and think of it as just one of the little ends of a long thread that reaches far beyond you and takes its place in the great, intricately woven pattern of a beautiful world. We do not see the whole pattern, but surely, surely, we know we are weaving it and that it is all spread out, beautiful and wonderful before the vision of the Almighty.

All work, too, absorbs some of the personality of the worker. You, weaving into the pattern of life your love and your interest, are sending out your personality into a wider world than you see. Any object handled or made by a person takes into itself some of the innermost nature of the maker, and holds it there; often it goes deeper and rises higher than he does. The very landscape round you, the room you sit in, become the revealers of yourself, with your secret passions, your hidden wishes, your hopes and your fears. If you want to know real things about people, go into the rooms they live and by the very objects they have gathered round them you will know them. So in all your work never fear to put in your love and your individuality. They will get there anyhow.

So whatever your work be, however narrow and limited, put your love into it first, and then imagination, and see how it will be transformed. We sow half-blindly and lo! how much greater is the garnering than the silent seeds we dropped into the soil.

But there is another reason for loving our work. There come moments to each and all of us when, as the phrase has it, we are "up against it." The absorbing affection is betrayed; the child for whom we have lived has failed; the fortune we have amassed has gone at one fell swoop—not one of us is out of reach of accident or safe from the hand of tragedy.

What, then, is the unfailing solace when the catastrophe has fallen? Believe me, it is the habit of work. That task which the world waits on us to do; that necessity for production which we shall only escape when the vital spark within us has slipped from its casement and gone off adventuring into the strange and new. Work calls to us still. It holds our mind from absorption in our loss, our disappointment and our grief and slowly by numbing the pain at first, it begins to heal the gash which sorrow has made, and sets us up again, maimed a little perhaps, but wiser and braver on the path of our recreated life.

Our work, whatever it be, bearing or training a child, making a home, or a book, or a garden, or a road, or a picture of a fertile field lives on when we are gone and speaks to those who follow us of our courage and our fidelity.

* * *

An optimist is one who can enjoy the larger part of the year merely by looking forward to her next vacation.

SEAGRASS RUNABOUT.
F1 134X.—Seagrass Runabout, artistically designed, and very comfortable; fitted with rubber tyres, has adjustable drop front
C. & F. PRICE **73/6**

How to Make Baby Happy

The mother may be expert in baby hygiene, baby feeding and baby diseases. She may be able to apply the last word in child welfare to the upbringing of her little one, but there is quite as vital a thought to be kept in mind in connection with baby lore.

We must keep the baby happy.

The little one comes into the world with as marvellously growing a mind and emotional nature as body. He feels joy and sunshine and love quite if not almost as keenly as he feels hunger. His gratitude for his mother's smile is as heartfelt as that which he feels for his bottle of warm food. How, then, can we bring the right kind of joy to our babies that they may grow up emotionally as well as bodily healthy?

The baby's physical comfort comes first as having an important relation to his mental health. The home that houses the baby should be sunny, well ventilated and dry. This is not always limited by the income of the family; it is a matter of selecting the sunny side of the street, the better arrangement of rooms, the better plumbing and the wider yard space for the same rental as less comfortable conditions. If it is necessary to select a city house, the parents should consider what possibilities of improvements it holds. Can the roof be utilized for play space? Is there available space for putting on a porch or bay window on one side? Can the back yard be made over adequately to hold simple apparatus—a swing, poles, ladder, balance beam, a sand pile—for the toddler's future physical development?

Parents who live in small communities or in the country will not have this important light and air consideration, but their housing precautions for the baby will be even more important. The basement or cellar should be dry. If the water supply comes from a well, the well should be so located that the water is not polluted by dangerous drainage from a stable or outhouse. Nearby piles of garbage, pools of stagnant water, manure heaps, refuse or rubbish of any kind are all a menace to babyhood and should be disposed of.

Sunshine makes the baby supremely happy. The little one basks and warms and unfolds in it just as does a flower. That room in which the sun shines the longest during the day should be used as the baby's living-room. The room should have a constant supply of fresh air, as the baby will be much less liable to illness than when he is deprived of it. To "air" a room at intervals by opening the windows is well, but a far better plan is to have a continual stream of fresh air flowing through. To do this the windows must be opened on opposite sides of the room in order to secure a cross draft, which is always necessary to real ventilation. When the outside temperature is so extremely low that a comfortable temperature cannot be maintained with the windows open, outside air should be frequently admitted by opening wide the windows on opposite sides and flushing every part of the room for a few moments. In severe weather it is a good plan to air the nursery whenever the baby is taken into another room. In all the mild months the windows should be kept constantly open night and day.

Although the baby flowers in the sunshine, care must be taken in his earlier months to prevent the eye strain that results from direct rays of light. The little one's eyes and head should be shielded from the direct sunlight, even when he is asleep. Neither should he be allowed to lie with his eyes turned directly toward the sky, even if it is a grey day. The window screens in a room occupied by a toddler should be so made as to lower from the top, or thin wooden slats should be used to keep the lower sash secure. All screens should be so securely fastened as to have no possibility of their being pushed out. And the greatest care should be taken to protect the little one from the discomfort and danger of flies and mosquitoes. If the house is not adequately screened, the baby's bed or carriage should be covered with netting. This should be arranged tent fashion, suspended over a crude, light framework that the little one may not have the discomfort that comes from the fabric touching his face.

We all know how dependent we are for comforting rest upon the right kind of bed. The baby's muscles are even more easily tired and cramped than ours and his bed needs to be exactly suited to his needs.

The first bed may be made from an ordinary clothes-basket or from a light box, such as a fruit case. Later a metal cot with a firm spring is desirable. A sanitary cot mattress may be made by stuffing bed ticking with kapok, which can be renewed as often as necessary. Sphagnum moss, or straw, can be used in the same way. The mattress cover may be made of bed ticking or heavy unbleached muslin, which can be emptied, washed, and dried in the sun at intervals.

It is almost impossible to gauge the discomfort and resultant peevishness that is caused in the body and mind of the baby by our frequent careless choice of his carriage. The folding pram, light and inexpensive, is valuable because it allows mother and baby to go to many places for air and play made impossible by a heavier vehicle. But these prams should be used only for such trips as are taken when the mother can hold the baby for a greater part of the way. Otherwise the little limbs will become cramped and real pain to the child follow.

The best baby carriage for general street and nursery use measures at least two feet from the ground. A carriage lower than this exposes the baby to driving currents of cold and hot air underneath that are not only uncomfortable but health menacing. He is also jeopardized by the germ-laden dust of the street in a lower vehicle. This high carriage should be roomy enough to hold under and upper wrappings and a comfortable pillow. It should also allow space for the baby to lie down without any resulting muscular strain. The top should be lined with green and be easily and quickly adjustable to meet any weather changes. Strong, well-balanced springs are necessary and the carriage should have wheels with rubber tyres. A strap is imperative, but if one can be arranged to adjust about the baby's waist, fastening at the back, this is more comfortable and efficacious than the ordinary carriage strap.

Next to baby's comfort in his best emotional development is the best home accommodation for his free, muscular play that develops him as almost nothing else does. A creeping pen affords the necessary protection to the baby and gives space for play. It consists of a fence made in four sections, each, say, 18 inches high and four feet long, hinged at three corners and latched at the fourth. Ready-made pens have spindles like a stair rail, so that baby may have something to take hold of when he strives to climb to his feet. As it folds together, the pen can be readily moved about. The floor of the pen should be made of something soft to save the baby from bumps. A cork mat is the cleanest and best material, but a blanket or rug will answer. When the pen is used in the yard a floor of clean white sand will not only protect the clothing, but afford the baby who is old enough to play by himself much wholesome entertainment.

When it is not possible to purchase one of the ready-made articles an ingenious person may devise a satisfactory play pen from any materials at hand. A board six or eight feet long and a foot wide may be used to fence off a sunny corner of the nursery for a pen.

Only a few well-chosen furnishings and toys are necessary for baby play. No child should use a high chair until his spine is strong and he is able to hold his head erect. The habit of leaving a very young child in a high chair, fastened and alone, for even a comparatively short period of time, is dangerous. The rigid sitting position may result in a permanent curvature of the spine. Toys should be large, washable and without sharp edges or points. Any toy that has loose parts such as tassels or bells that can be loosed, and possibly swallowed, should be tabooed. The same rule holds in connection with those toys that are painted or have a woolly covering. A light basket covered with oilcloth that can be easily washed may be used to hold clothes-pins, blocks, spools for stringing, a spoon or two and the other simple home objects that delight a child in its early months just as much as do the more elaborate and expensive toys. This basket and its contents may be easily and frequently washed and it will furnish the baby with endless delight.

The baby who is good is the happy baby. The right kind of home discipline for the child of this early age will not only keep the baby joyful but will help to establish his mental health, for a cross baby often results in a sick or ailing one. Often our thoughtless playing with the baby irritates him. A young, delicate baby needs a good deal of rest, alone. We love to hear him laugh and crow in what we think is delight as we tickle, punch or toss the frail little body, but his resulting glee is usually caused by nervousness, and irritability is bound to follow. The baby should not be rocked, jumped up and down, tossed, shaken or jounced in his cot or carriage. To rest and change the position of his body he should be taken up occasionally and held in his mother's arms, but quietly, and only to rest his muscles.

An older child should be taught to sit on the floor or in his pen or cot during part of his waking hours, or he will be very likely to make too great demands upon the mother's strength. No one who has not tried it realizes how much nervous energy can be consumed in "minding" a baby who can creep or walk about, and who must be continually watched and diverted, and the mother who is taking the baby through this period of life will need to conserve all her strength, and not waste it in useless forms of activity.

When a baby cries simply because he has learned from experience that this brings him what he wants, it is one of the worst habits he can learn, and one which takes all the strength of the mother to break. Crying should cease when the cause has been removed. If the baby cries persistently for no apparent cause, the mother may suspect illness, pain, hunger or thirst. But if finally, after careful scrutiny of all these conditions, no cause for the crying can be found, the baby probably wants to be taken up, walked with, played with, rocked, or to have a light, or to have someone sit by him—the result of his having learned that crying will get him what he wants, and sufficient to make a spoiled, fussy baby, and a household tyrant whose continual demands make a slave of the mother. It is difficult to break up this habit after it has been formed, but it can be done. After the baby's needs have been fully satisfied he should be put down alone and allowed to cry until he goes to sleep. This may sound cruel, and it is very hard for a young mother to do, but it will usually take only a few nights of this discipline to accomplish the result. In some cases persistent crying may be due to causes not readily discernible by the mother; in this event, the opinion of a good doctor as to the cause of the crying should be sought.

Thumb-sucking is another habit that needs attention. To break it up requires resolution and patience on the part of the mother. The thumb or finger must be persistently and constantly removed from the mouth and baby's attention diverted to something else. The sleeve may be pinned or sewed down over the fingers of the offending hand for several days and nights, or the hand may be put in a cotton mitten. The baby's hands should be set free now and then, especially if he is old enough to use his hands for his toys, and at meal times, to save as much unnecessary strain on his nerves as possible, but with the approach of sleeping time the hand must be covered.

A good deal of the naughtiness of babyhood has its beginnings in physical discomfort. Babies who are properly fed, who are kept hygienically clean, who sleep and play comfortably in plenty of fresh air and who have been properly trained, are happy, well-behaved babies. The period of infancy is more important than any later two years of life. The child's nervous system is like a series of telegraph wires carrying impulses through the eyes, ears, fingers and mouth to the brain—each impulse making a deeper habit path for itself than the last.

* * *

A thoroughbred doesn't need much whipping. He does his best. You?

* * *

We can be happy without a fortune, but not without friends.

How to be Graceful

Any woman can be graceful who learns her own defects and how to hide them, and who knows her own beauties and how to make the most of them. This is what the life of the stage teaches the actress. It's a secret which has given actresses a reputation for beauty. If any woman will watch a few good actresses carefully, through a number of impersonations, she will discover the secret of their charm, and she will subconsciously learn the lesson which the actress, in turn, is learning from the stage director.

You will observe that it generally is the clever actress who is graceful. That is because she has brains enough to accept the director's training. She knows that he bids her stand in some certain way because some good line of her body is thereby thrown into prominence. If the actress herself possesses the artistic eye and the gift of impersonal analysis; if she can, figuratively speaking, place the various sections of her body on the model's pedestal, and study them as a student does a lay figure, she soon learns each good line in her composition, and endeavors to utilize it most advantageously.

Few women know how to sit down properly. Observe the women in the next tram-car you enter, as they sit down. One flops down limply, one lolls; another sits hunched; a stout women sits gingerly on the edge as if afraid to trust the seat to bear her weight, and fully half of the young women and girls are painfully conscious of their hands and feet. The woman who sits down gracefully and retains her poise is rare indeed.

The actress learns to place her foot firmly but lightly on the floor, and to sway her body from one side to another, without lifting her foot. As one director ably commanded, "Put your feet on the floor and leave them there." Sureness on the feet is the first lesson which women can learn from women of the stage. Note that actresses firmly but lightly put the ball of the foot down first, and that they never make futile, uncertain little motions of the feet. If they are standing still, they stand; if they are walking, they walk. Their actions are definite and exact.

When you walk, swing the leg from the hip, instead of from the knee, as too many women do. Breathe deeply; keep your mind upon the good rather than upon the evil of life; and in a month you will laugh at physical ills and mental distresses, and you will have begun, at least, to be graceful. The woman who holds her chest up never complains of an increasing waistline. The muscles are held too taut, too firmly, for that to happen. It is only when the waist muscles are allowed to sag, which drops the chest down upon the stomach and deprives the shoulders of their carrying power, that we find the enemy, fat, gaining a hold.

All forms of directed exercise make for grace. A woman who wishes to be beautiful in the use of her body should learn to dance, to swim, and above all to use her muscles well in the ordinary actions of life. When you are stooping to dust the rounds of a chair, do not bend over rigidly from the waist, but bend your knees slightly, and flex the whole body toward the point where your hand is. When you sweep, grasp the handle of the broom firmly, step briskly and accurately in its path as you sweep, and be careful to hold up your shoulders. No sport in the world has a more beneficial effect upon womanly grace than the prosaic work of sweeping.

Never loll in a chair. If you wish to rest, lie back in it, pressing your back firmly against the support, relaxing your hands, and finding a comfortable place for your head. When you sleep, stretch your limbs out fully, and lie down —that is, lie so that you actually feel the support of the bed beneath you. This method will relax your muscles.

A good carriage has much to do with success in acquiring grace. Never mind about your shoulders; they will fall naturally into their place if the chest is correctly held. The woman who holds her chest up will glance at you pityingly when you speak of indigestion, backache, and similar physical worries.

The secret of health is to adjust all the parts of your machine. Lift your chest, and all the other organs in your body will slip into the place Nature designed for them. Learn to hold your chest forward in walking, even straining against it, as a horse strains against a harness. Hold your head easily balanced on your shoulders.

Crossing the arms gracefully is an art that never seems to be understood outside the theatre. Most women who assume this position fold the hands down inside the arms. The hands should be laid out straight, one crossing the right arm and the other just holding to the left.

To avoid self-consciousness, learn certain fundamental rules, and think of them as abstractions. Don't try to make your gestures with indefinite, exaggerated movements of the hands, but begin by training your hands to express simply and naturally what you feel. A hand absolutely at rest, relaxed, and comfortable, is always a graceful hand. When uncertain about any particular gesture remember that, and just let them rest. You never saw a pianist with awkward hands. You never saw a skilful dancer with awkward feet. You never saw a long-distance walker move about a room awkwardly.

The requirements for the lesson of grace, therefore, are, first, a knowledge of your own limitations, and then a training of the members of the body. After these is required the final touch of a serene, kindly and sincere mind, which will render the glance limpid, compose the face, and give dignity to the carriage.

* * *

Even the meanest woman isn't always as mean as she is sometimes!

* * *

Don't worry. A woman who has worried all her life hasn't anything to show for it, except wrinkles.

* * *

Every day is a dull day for dull people.

* * *

The best valentine is kindness all year round.

Do not Worry!

Anxiety and worry kill in us one of our greatest sources of happiness—namely, the power of observation. The worrier is like a person who will look at the speck on the window, instead of at the view beyond. What sort of a world is this to one who never sees the sun set in winged flames, or the moon rise cool and round over the eastern edge of a surging ocean, flinging an argent pathway to the shore? What sort of a world is it to the man who has so many anxieties that he does not see the cloud shadows, blue and violet and deep purple, shifting over the distant mountains?

To have lived missing all the shifting scenery of the sky, all the multi-colored beauty of the earth, all the august dignity and fine enwrapping majesty of human nature, is worse than to have lived without a full supply of bread and meat and clothing. Remember this when you walk over snow-clad hills.

You remember Jesus Christ warned against worry when He spoke of the lilies of the field, that toil not neither do they spin, when He assured us that not a sparrow falleth to the ground but "my Father which is in heaven" knoweth it. I have thought about that a good deal, for certainly, the world being adjusted as it is now, it is hardly fair to suggest to young persons just starting out in life that if they toil not, neither do they spin, they will somehow get taken care of and will not fall to the ground. The more I thought of it the more I believed that what this one great example meant was, "Don't worry." The lilies do not worry, and yet they blossom. The sparrows do not worry, and yet they find food; and if indeed they fall to the ground, that, too, is all in the general scheme of life.

So of human beings: it is not necessary that we take thought what we should eat or what we should drink, or what we should do to be paid for it, but we must simply realize that this is a world of service. We must choose a mode of service and try to carry it out better each year, and our power to help will give us our place and our rewards.

Life is just the stuff that tests the metal you are made of. You must fall into the hands of thieves and liars, of cowards and hypocrites. The best you can do about it is to decide firmly that you will not be like them. But also do not worry about them. They bear in themselves the seed of their own extinction.

Do you remember in the wonderful series of the "Chronicles of Barsetshire" by Anthony Trollope, the pathetic figure of Mr. Crawley? Mr. Crawley was perpetual curate in the small village of Hogglestock. His salary was far too small for two people to live on, much less his family of four. He was a learned man, who read the "Odes" of Horace and the Plays of Euripides in the original, and yet he was set apart to minister to bricklayers.

Finally, he was accused—he, a gentleman of high learning and refinement—of stealing twenty pounds, and was not only to be tried by the civil courts, but by an ecclesiastical inquiry. One day pending the trial he sat out on a stone in the drizzling rain thinking it over, when one of his old bricklayers came by, and laying his hand on his shoulder he said: "Tell 'ee what, Mister Crawley, and yer Reverence mustn't think I means to be preachin': there ain't nowt a man can't bear if he'll only be dogged. . . . It's dogged as does it. It ain't thinkin' about it."

Now there is a bit of true wisdom about life—"It isn't thinkin' about it." Worrying will get you nowhere, unless it is into a hospital. "But it's dogged as does it." You go on steadily day after day working toward a given end, and ultimately, perforce, you will find yourself nearer to that end.

I know of a woman who when she was a young girl set as a motto over her desk: "Bear it out, even to the edge of Doom."

But when she grew to be thirty or thereabouts, and she realized how universal is this struggle with the uprising evil in life, how each one has his burden to bear and his stand to make, she tore down the motto, laughing, and put in its stead:

" 'Tis dogged as does it."

Indecision is a soul diesase, just as trembling and twitching is a bodily disease.

There was an old saying in medieval times that the knight who would win the treasure must never look around. So it is after making a resolution. Make up your mind as slowly and carefully as you can, and having made it up, never look round again. You have chosen your treasure; you know the direction in which it lies; go steadily toward it; banish all worry and all anxiety, and remember,

" 'Tis dogged as does it."

"I Must Say I Enjoy Life."

"Life," said a gaunt widow, with a reputation for being clever—"life is a perpetual toothache."

In this vein the conversation went on; the familiar topics were discussed of labor troubles, epidemics, tuberculosis, and taxation.

Near me there sat a little old lady who was placidly drinking her tea, and taking no part in the melancholy chorus. "Well, I must say," she remarked, turning to me and speaking in an undertone, "I must say I enjoy life."

"So do I," I whispered.

"When I enjoy things," she went on, "I know it. Eating, for instance, the sunshine, my hot-water bottle at night. Other people are always thinking of unpleasant things. It makes a difference," she added, as she got up to go with the others.

"All the difference in the world," I answered.

Etiquette *for* Guests

If your best friend were to tell you, as you were about to journey to another town to become the guest of a dear friend, to look out for the "twenty guest failures," you would doubtless be considerably puzzled until she explained that there are a score of ordinary little things the average guest does, for the most part unthinkingly, that are, nevertheless, unpleasant for the hostess.

Every woman who has entertained company knows full well that she delights in entertaining some of her friends, and no matter whether they stay two days or three weeks, she always hates to have them go. On the other hand, there are other friends of whom she is quite fond in a general way, and yet the moment they become her guests there is a something about them and their methods that are not quite pleasant. The reason for this is undoubtedly in the fact that they do one or more of the twenty things that guests should not do. Here are the twenty:

Never "drop in" on a friend unexpectedly. Give her at least a little notice, even if you have to telegraph or telephone, and if you are invited, be sure and let her know the day and hour you expect to arrive, and just how you expect to arrive.

Unless you are going to spend an entire summer of three months as the guest of a friend, never take more than one trunk, and preferably a small one at that. You can pack your toilet articles and sleeping garments in your travelling bag, and you can get sufficient clothes in the medium-sized trunk for all needs for a period of anywhere from one to eight weeks. Furthermore, do not forget to put your sleeping garment in your travelling bag. Otherwise you will have to get them from your hostess in case your trunk is not delivered on the day of your arrival, which every travelling woman knows very frequently happens.

If the day is pleasant go ahead and talk about it. Praise the weather, tell how you enjoy it, but if the weather

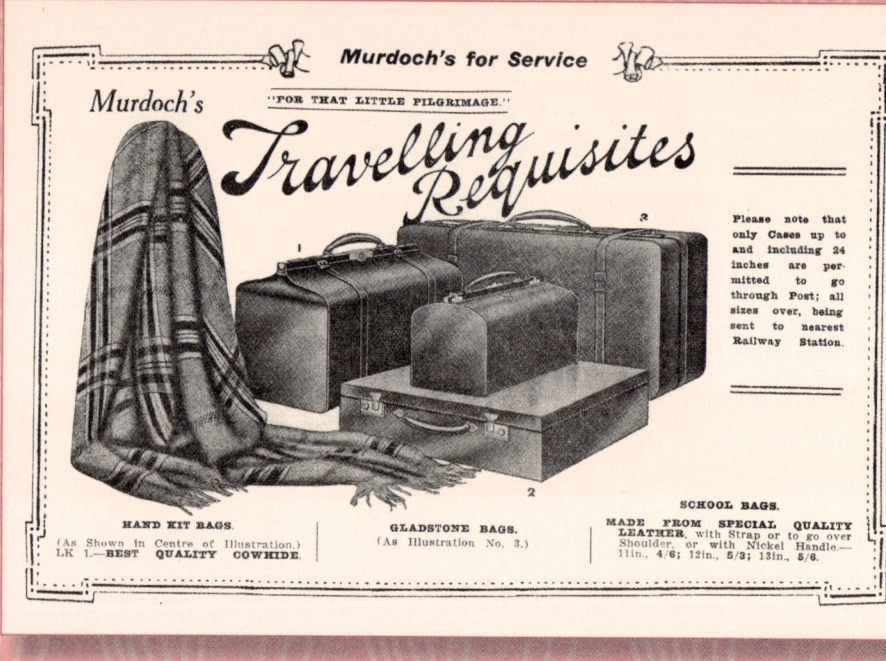

be unpleasant do not make any further comment upon it than to say it is raining. Do not say that it is miserable weather and you always feel badly when it is rainy, or otherwise grumble about the weather, for this does not add to the comfort of your hostess one iota; rather, it makes her feel as though your visit was not pleasing you. Half a moment's reflection should suffice to convince you that your hostess is not in any manner whatever responsible for the weather.

If you remain long as a guest in the average household a little domestic unpleasantness is very likely to occur. No man or woman is absolutely perfect. Something may displease the host or hostess, and they may have a quiet word or two about it. Never under any consideration in the wide, wide world enter into any such conversation, never make any comments to either the host or hostess, and, above all, never appear to notice these things.

If you are invited to stay two weeks do not stay a day over two weeks. When your time is up your hostess will, of course, ask you to stay longer. She may mean it and be sincere about it, but unless something happens in the household where your presence would be a help, always make your departure at the specified time. If you make a practice of this you will be doubly welcome the next time. Bear in mind that your hostess may have plans she would like to carry out as soon as you leave, and if you do not leave on the specified time you may interfere with these plans.

If you are at a friend's house for any length of time there are always a number of little bills to be paid. There may be telegraph charges or telephone charges. Then there are express bills, and laundry bills, and various other little bills. Make sure every one of these is paid before you go away.

No matter how well supplied your room may be with toilet articles, always bring your own. This includes everything for the toilet excepting, of course, towels, and one or two towels may also be taken in case you should spill any of your toilet waters or face powders, as it would not be proper to use your hostess' linen for cleaning up such things.

Another thing every guest should remember to take with her is a plentiful supply of her own stationery and postage stamps. Too many guests sit down at their hostess' writing desk and make free with her stationery and stamps. This is exceedingly bad form. A woman's stationery is generally a personal matter which she buys to suit herself, and, of course, you know that postage stamps are the same as money.

If there are servants in the house where you are visiting, never embarrass your host or hostess by tipping them freely on every occasion. You are not in a hotel and you should take it for granted that your friends pay their servants a sufficient wage. At the end of your visit, however, it is all right to remember each servant, or at least such servants as you come in daily contact with, like the parlor maid, butler, chauffeur, etc., etc. Leave either a little present or a small sum of money for them when you go.

You may be visiting in a city or town where you have other acquaintances of whom you are exceedingly fond, but while you are the guest of one friend you should do no more than pay a call on your other friends. Never by any means stay over night with them, and, above all, do not invite them to dinner with you.

No matter how careless you may be in your own home in regard to leaving your things about, it is quite a different thing when you are visiting. At your own home you may have a maid who will pick up the magazine you left on the couch or the kimono you left in the middle of your sleeping-room, but when visiting take care of these things yourself. Do not leave your wraps lying about the house, nor your books or other personal belongings scattered here and there. You may leave your embroidery on the verandah, a magazine on the lawn and other things scattered about. This means so much extra work for your friend or her servant.

There is another habit many guests have, if they are accustomed to go about visiting now and then, and it is a grievously bad habit—and that is telling your host and hostess what a beautiful place "so and so" has. Do not say that Mr. Smith has a wonderful garden, or the drawing-room in Mrs. Jones's home is perfectly exquisite. In fact, do not comment at all upon the homes and belongings of other friends other than to say that they seem to be quite happy and comfortable for such expiation upon the homes of others is likely to make your hostess feel as though you were drawing comparisons in which her own home by no means took the lead.

Be ten times as careful of your hostess' belongings as you would of your own. If you come back dusty from an automobile ride do not rush indoors and wipe the dust from your face with your friend's best monogramed linen. Take a face cloth or a cheaper towel for this. Never brush the dust from your shoes with your friend's towels. This seems absurd advice, but it is frequently done.

The servants of your hostess are employed by her to do her bidding. When she requests them to attend to you, that is quite right, but under no consideration should you order her servants about.

Before you have been in the home of your friend more than two days you will get an idea of when they have their meals. Always be on time. By all means get down to breakfast with your host and hostess. If you have ever entertained friends you know how disagreeable it is to have to wait for breakfast. Perhaps your husband is in a hurry to get away, and you expect to get up any minute for your guests. Remember this, and always be prompt at meal time.

If there are children where you are visiting never make the grave error of telling how perfectly well trained your sister's or cousin's or other friend's child is. No matter how incorrigible your hostess' children may be or how much like angels they are, any comment upon the good qualities of other people's children is decidedly out of place and impolite.

If you go to the theatre or some other place and come back late at night do not enter the house noisily, chattering and laughing for there are other people in the household who have rights and should not be disturbed. You would not do this in your own home, nor should you do it when visiting.

There are women who go visiting and buy little things for their hostess' table such as fruits, and other dainties. This is the height of impoliteness, and is really an insult, as it is an intimation that you are not getting sufficient foods either in quantity or quality.

Do not give pennies or any money to the children. If you want them to have a little present consult their mother as to what to get them. If you want to give them money give it to their mother for them. The chances are their mother doesn't want them to spend money and she may be greatly disturbed if the children are given a little change with which they may buy the oft-times unwholesome penny candy.

Never appear uneasy while visiting. Do not stroll to the windows or doors and look out longingly, giving the impression that you are getting deadly dull and feel as though you were imprisoned. Do not say, "Oh, dear, I wonder what I will do to-day."

If the guest will remember all these things, she will find that wherever she has visited she will be doubly welcome next time and that year after year she will be fairly deluged with invitations from her friends begging her to make them a visit.

Ask a man to wink, and he will invariably do so with his weakest eye. With men this is generally the left eye, just as, with men, the left ear is the weakest and is least able to resist trouble or deafness. With women the tendency to weakness in the left eye or left ear is less.

How to Care for Your Hair

The main trouble with hair is that we interfere so much with Nature and so unintelligently. All she wants us to do is to keep our hair clean and give it a little exercise.

Don't wash any oftener than once a month and exercise by brushing rather than massage.

If you are one of those persons who thinks you have to wash your hair every week, wash it in lukewarm water, not hot. The weekly shampoo with hot water weakens the glands in the scalp so that they expand and do not contract actively, then the oil overflows, and you have excessively oily hair for several inches from the scalp, and then dry and brittle ends; a weekly shampoo also keeps the pores of the scalp wide open and the impurities of the body—oils and so on—go out through those open pores and make the hair greasy and clinging. It takes very strong hair to stand a weekly shampoo—better take treatments in connection with it—tonic or intelligent massage.

There is a better way, we think, to keep your hair clean than washing it every week. Have two good brushes and wash one of them every day—brushing your hair with a dirty brush is inhuman treatment to one of your best friends. Your brush should have long flexible bristles, for they are the only kind that will thoroughly cleanse the hair and not break it. Then get a cleansing tonic—pour a little tonic in a saucer, take absorbent cotton about three inches square and, wadding it up, make a sort of sponge of it; now brush your hair out with the brush you've been using; then part the hair, beginning in the centre, and make the parts not over three-quarters of an inch apart; dip your cotton sponge in the tonic, squeeze it out a little so that the tonic won't go all over the hair, and rub it lightly on the parts. When you have got it all over your head, take a soft hand-towel and dry your head just as you do after a shampoo. Never use a Turkish towel. It breaks the hair and it leaves lint.

When your hair is almost dry, give your scalp a little massage to get the circulation up and the scalp loose—a tight scalp means an undernourished topknot; then take your clean brush, holding it firmly by the back just behind the bristles not by the long handle, but almost as a military brush is held—this gives a better stroke and accomplishes more in the brushing. Separate your hair into strands and brush, always brushing upward and outward from the scalp not down flat against it, and brush with long strokes that go to the end of your hair.

The cleansing tonic can be used every day if the hair is in very bad condition, either too oily or too dry or sick with dandruff. But if your hair is normally healthy, use the tonic only once or twice a week, but brush every day. Brushing not only cleanses the hair and of the impurities the scalp sends off, but it polishes it and gives gloss.

Each must find out for herself the best way for her hair, we suppose. But we believe in the shampoo every three months as firmly as we do in ultimate salvation for everybody because our own topknot got cured that way and also got curly. When we took our dying tresses to a place we know about, they were like an oily cap. We had tried violet ray, weekly shampoo, 'n'ever'thing, and we just got worse and worse. When they told us we couldn't wash our hair for three months and if we tried to cheat or slip in a little shampoo before that time we needn't come back to them, we thought we had to go into exile somewhere until we served our term, but it wasn't a month before our hair began to be fluffy and once more friendly to our face; and in two months it was the way it used to be in the nice days of our youth, fluffy, and the lights come back into it, and a little pleasant, healthy curl added to it.

Nature made it and understands it, and she'll take care of it if you don't hinder her and are willing to help her a little in a world that is full of a kind of dirt and destruction she didn't count on when she started in on hair —motor and factories and tenser living. "Keep it clean and exercise it by brushing."

Hair also needs a little oil as food when people live tensely and nervously. The skin of a nervous person is usually dry all over face and head and body. And hair that has much water on it decidedly needs oil foods to take the place of the natural food that is washed out.

The reason dandruff is so common is that it is a germ and contagious. There are two kinds of dandruff—the kind that is as fine as powder and can't be seen, and the kind that shows thick and scaly and falls about one's shoulders. The first is serious and hard to overcome. It causes irritation and falling hair. It can be cured by the right kind of lotion—there are too many. Beware of the spurious ones; one place cures it by removing the epidermis with iodid. The second kind of dandruff is not so harmful, and far more easily cured. A great percentage of so-called dandruff cases are merely a dry skin which peels off the scalp. This is caused by acidity, indigestion, or irritations where the dust has collected on the scalp and has to be washed off every week or ten days instead of being brushed out daily.

We have said that the hair has a health all of its own quite independent of the health of the body; that's true; but just as no part of you is utterly free from any other part of you, just so fever, nervous strain, general exhaustion do affect the hair; they affect the circulation. Massage—the right kind of massage—gives relaxation, loosens the scalp, brings good circulation to the roots.

Great caution should be used in finding proper tonics. Tonics are good to bolster up the hair through any bad time and cleansing tonics are almost essential in these enlightened days of dust and despair. It is not generally known among the public, probably, but denatured alcohol is being used in many tonics nowadays. It is free of tax and therefore extremely cheap. There are manufacturers of tonics who claim that wood alcohol is a disinfectant, but it is nevertheless a terrible poison and risky to use where there may be an abrasion of the skin or scalp. Only the smallest amount of alcohol possible is put in the best hair tonics.

Then there is this little matter of dyeing. As we grow older, our hair fades, we miss the lights in it, but dyeing is a very tricky affair. Though we may not know it, our skin loses its high lights, too, and Nature, the blessed old artist she is, fades harmoniously hair and skin and eyes together. The art of coloring the hair is to keep in harmony with your face and eyes. Stick to the natural coloring as closely as possible.

And now back to curls. If your hair has a little bit of curl in it, get a waving lotion, only be sure that it is not a harmful one, and a set of combs, and while you're reading your morning chapter in the best book in the world or doing the dishes or manicuring your nails take a bit of absorbent cotton and dampen your hair with the lotion; then put your combs in, six or eight of them, where you want the ripples to come and let them stay until the hair dries. You'll have a lovely soft wave not so stiff and artificial as the usual marcel. After you have done this a few times you'll find the wave staying by you through thick and thin.

Permanent waving with the machine is not destructive if it is done exactly right. If you're going to be permanent-waved, you ought to know fully as much about your waver as you should about the man whom you are going to take on for life. We have found that most people who have a permanent wave every six months or a year have dead-looking hair, no softness and no lovely lights, but it is possible to keep both if you have a safe waver and good tonics.

Follow the fashion if you like, but always adapt it to your face—look at your nose and the curve of your chin and the line from your shoulder to your neck and the side of your head. When you look at yourself, you see only one, possibly two, angles—everybody else sees your whole head. You may be doing your hair so that it is very nice front view or profile but the line of the whole head is

faulty. Not only must you think of your whole head but your body as well; if you are short, your hair should be dressed so as to make your head small, unless, of course, you are fat. The charm of hair is its softness and gleam. Simple shining hair like a soft, befriending frame around the face, is the thing that stirs poets into lyrics and lovers into matrimony.

Bobbed or long, it doesn't matter—make your hair the kind that belongs to your type. Don't be content with tight, slinky, horrid old hair done up any old way. Give it a chance to show what a good friend it can be. As a matter of fact, it is the second-best friend your face has— the first is that inside you, the thing that is back of your face.

1. The way to wash your hair: Always let the water run over it from the spray thoroughly before you put any soap on it. Use pure soaps, shaved off, and boiled with water until dissolved. Never rub a cake of soap on the hair. Then wash in water that is not too hot, rinse in the bowl, then wash again with soap, and rinse in at least two bowls of clear water before you spray it. Keep on spraying long after you think you have sprayed enough. The main difficulty with washing your own hair is that you don't get the soap out. Dry in the sun if possible.

2. The way to wash brushes: The proper care of a good brush is almost as essential as the use of it. It should be washed almost every time it is used. Swish it through warm water and soap suds made from a good plain soap; rinse well in warm water, then cold, and dry in the open air. This care will double the life of any brush.

3. The way to massage: Massage with the base of the palm, steadying the palms by the fingers pressed lightly but firmly on the scalp. Do not let the palms move but hold them firmly and move the scalp in a circular motion always up from the face instead of down toward the face. Never press hard with the fingers.

SAVE!

Wisdom in Housekeeping Makes for Happiness in Home Life

SAVE THE KITCHEN FLOOR.

Pieces of "rubber matting" put in front of the table and the sink, the two places where people are most likely to stand, are a valuable aid toward keeping the kitchen hardwood floor in good condition. Their elasticity is easy for the feet, they can be carried out and washed absolutely clean with the hose, they lessen the noise of the delivery men and they save many a scratch and track on the clean floor. In our case, this matting was found in a catalogue, although it may be had from the hardware store.

SAVE ON BRUSHES.

Brushes should be hung up. They should never be allowed to stand on their bristles as this mats them and tends to make the bristles fall out. In using a broom, sometimes use one side and sometimes the other; this will make it wear evenly and so last longer. An oil mop will wear longer if it is not hung too near the heat after washing it. The bristles of a carpet-sweeper or a vacuum cleaner can be well cleaned of hairs with a button-hook or a pair of scissors.

SAVE ON BUCKETS.

Buckets have only regular handles. To pour the contents from a bucket is not an agreeable thing to do. One hand must be used to grasp the bottom, which is usually hot. A wooden hoop with a handle attached will prevent burning the hands and also aid in the lifting.

Take a hoop from an old barrel, soak it in warm water, then bend it to fit the bottom of the bucket, rivet it together, make a handle out of a piece of round iron, flatten the ends and punch holes to join.

This can be fitted to the bottom and removed as desired. It makes a very handy device for a bucket to be used on wash-days, and will repay any one for the making.

SAVE ON BENZINE.

Don't throw away the benzine or gasoline you have used for cleaning, no matter how dirty it looks. Place in a covered jar, and in a little while the dirt or sediment will settle at the bottom and the benzine can be poured off and used afresh.

SAVE TABLE LINEN.

When fruit juice is spilt on table linen, sprinkle at once with salt to prevent a permanent stain.

SAVE ON SHOES.

Remember these things: When the shoes get wet be careful, in drying them, not to place them too near the fire, as they will burn almost instantly; and if dried too quickly, the life is taken out of the leather and its durability is destroyed. Also stuff wet shoes with paper or shoe-trees to prevent cracking and to keep the shape of the shoes. If your shoes are polished with proper dressing, they will wear twice as long as shoes that are not properly cared for. To keep them soft and pliable, there is nothing better than an oil which can be bought cheaply. Frequent applications of this oil—which is used in the Army—say once a week, will keep the leather soft; it will also add long life to the shoes. It should be applied to uppers and soles.

SAVE ON STOCKINGS.

Do you ever get discouraged when you find your leisure time is merely darning time? There will be less darning and a longer life to stockings if you buy them plenty large enough. This gives space for the foot to slide and saves much wear.

Silk stockings will wear much longer if they are laundered every day, for perspiration left in silk rots it. Make a warm (not hot) suds from a mild soap or soap flakes. Squeeze the suds through the stockings, rubbing as little as possible. Then turn the stockings inside out and squeeze the water through again, to make sure they are thoroughly clean. Wring gently. When almost dry, iron with a warm (not hot) iron.

Use two cups of salt to a gallon of cold water to set the color in black stockings that have a tendency to run. This may have to be used before every washing for stockings of this kind.

SAVE WEAR AROUND BUTTONS.

Mending the holes made by the tearing out of a button is usually a difficult task. An efficient way, particularly for children's clothes, is to sew the new button to a square of material similar to that of the torn garment, so as to leave it attached to a square of cloth larger than the hole to be repaired. Push the button through the hole from the back. The attached square of material will form a patch on the underside. Fell this down, catching the torn edges of the holes as you sew.

This makes a neat darn and also serves as a reinforcement. In making children's clothes where the buttons are especially apt to be torn out, it is a good idea to run an extra strip of material, or a piece of tape under where the buttons are to be. Then when the buttons are sewed on, the stitches should go through the double thickness.

SAVE ON FINE CHINA.

Fine china nicks particularly easily when it is warm. A towel in the bottom of the dish-pan will save much danger of chipping. Use a mild soap in washing painted or gilt-edged china and wash one piece at a time. Much fine china, especially that which is made in China, is rough on the bottom. Soft paper, or blanket-stitched flannel pads should be kept between dishes with rough backs to prevent the decoration on the front from being scratched, worn or chipped. Avoid using water that is too hot, in washing dishes, and put plates out edgewise, so that both sides will expand with the heat alike.

SAVE YOUR HANDS.

When you get paint or varnish on your hands pour a little kerosene oil on them, rub well and it will disappear at once. I find it better and more convenient than turpentine.

SAVE ON SHIRTS.

One way to lengthen the life of a man's shirt is this: Before ironing the bosom, cut a small piece from the bottom of the shirt, dip it in cold starch and place it under the worn spot where the corners of the collar rub the shirt. Iron at once. The adhesion will remain until the shirt is washed again, when the process can be repeated, using the same piece of material.

SAVE TIME ON DRESSING FOWLS.

After the large feathers are picked off, put your fowl into a pan of moderately-heated water, then with a case-knife scrape from the neck downward, and your fowl will be clean and white in one-fourth the time it would take in the old way of picking the small feathers out one at a time.

SAVE THE COTTON BAGS.

Cotton bags, used by millers, are very useful to homemakers for clothing, draperies and various household purposes. The manufacturers are now using printers' ink, which does not easily wash out, and house-keepers are perplexed to know how to make the same use of bags that they have in the past. A manufacturer gives us this method by which some bags may be utilized without an advertisement appearing on the surface of the garment.

Lay the bag out on the table and cover all the printing with a thin layer of common lard. After all the printed parts have been covered roll the sack up. After it has lain for the three days, it should then be unrolled and washed in boiling water. The lard having loosened the ink, the printing will immediately boil out and there will be a clean sack.

SAVE THE STOVE.

A soft, clean cloth dipped in melted paraffin will give the stove a smooth, attractive surface. Kerosene-oil on a soft lintless cloth may be used on the nickel afterward to effect a polish.

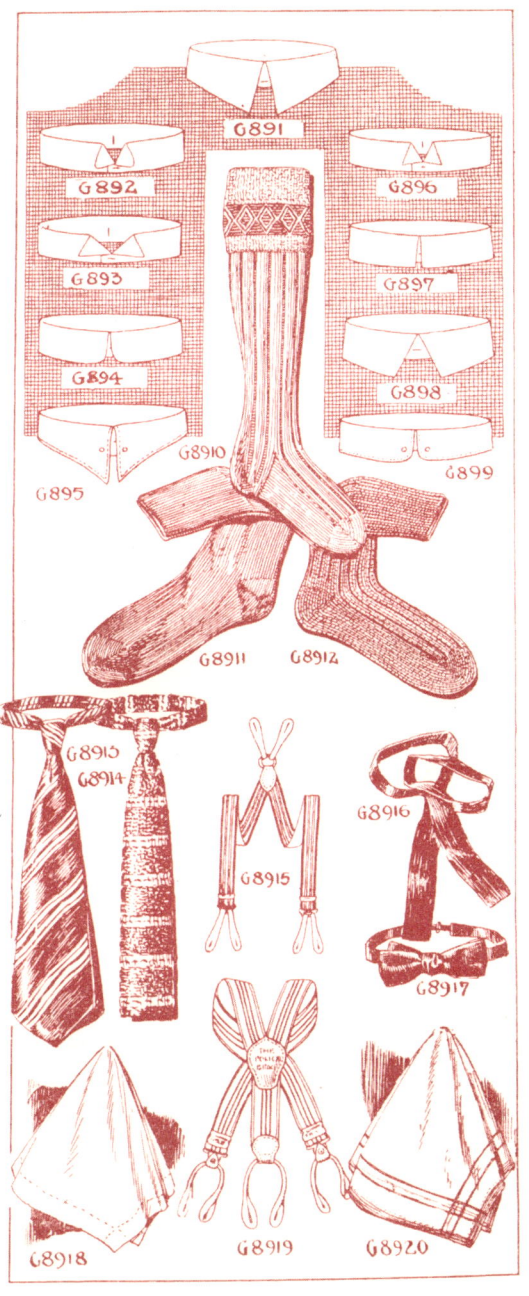

SAVE OLD STOCKINGS.

Home-made dustless mops from old stockings: Cut the straw from an old broom even with the wires that hold the straw together below the handle. Cover this part of the broom with an old stocking. Cut the legs of other old stockings into twelve-inch lengths and slash to within about two inches of the top in one-inch strips. Sew these strips to the covering of the broom in rows about one inch apart, until the mop is the desired thickness. Dip the mop into a solution made of half a cupful of melted paraffin and one cupful of kerosene, and allow the mixture to dry on. To keep the mop moist, roll it tightly and press it into a paper bag. Use this mop on oiled or polished floors. Without the dressing it may be used to wipe ceilings and walls.

When discarding children's hose, save all the good heels; they can be used to patch other heels that have holes too large to darn.

When children's ribbed stockings are hopelessly worn out, unravel the remaining parts of the legs, wind the cotton or wool on a spool and use for darning other stockings.

SAVE ON MEAT.

One way to cut down your meal bill is to prepare relatively small quantities of meat in such a way that the flavor is given to other and cheaper foods. For instance, it may be ground and combined with rice or bread crumbs to form croquettes; made into pies with relatively large quantities of pastry; cooked with dumplings; served in the same dish with gravy or with starch foods such as spaghetti and rice; ground and used with bread crumbs or other materials as a stuffing for vegetables such as tomatoes and green peppers; or cut thin and wrapped around a stuffing of bread crumbs or rice.

SAVE THE CAULIFLOWER LEAVES.

The large leaves of the cauliflower have a taste which is half-way between Brussels sprouts and young cabbage, and are altogether a pleasant surprise. They need about half an hour's boiling and may be served with butter, with cream sauce or with meat gravy.

SAVE CELERY TOPS.

Celery should be carefully bought with the two-way cooking in mind. If the hearts are bought, a very high price is paid whereas just as much of the vegetable for table use can be secured by buying the less fancy stalks, in which the tops are much longer and can used for creamed celery. In making this dish, be sure to put in quite a number of the whiter leaves, which add pungency to the flavor.

SAVE ON TABLE-CLOTHS.

Table-cloths will wear longer if, when ironed, they are folded in three parts one week and in four the next one.

SAVE ON SOAP.

Does soap seem to disappear in your house? If you will purchase a larger quantity of soap at a time, remove the wrapper, and allow the soap to "dry out" before using it, it will not dissolve so rapidly when placed in hot water and each cake will last much longer.

Save your small pieces of toilet soap, cut them up fine, put on to boil in cold water until all the soap is dissolved, then stir in enough corn meal to make it thick. Pour into tins to cool; when cold, cut into cakes.

SAVE ON GLOVES.

To mend a kid glove, place a bit of court-plaster, as nearly as possible the same shade as the glove, on the under-side of the torn part. Then bring the edges neatly together over it. This will not tear out as do stitches. Or place a thin piece of muslin on the wrong side, hold it securely in place, and stitch on the right side several times on the sewing machine. A glove which is mended in this way usually lasts until the remainder of the glove has completely worn out.

SAVE ON VINEGAR.

One quart of vinegar can make two by putting the two half-quarts into quart jars, filling up the jars with boiling water, screwing on the tops and letting stand for

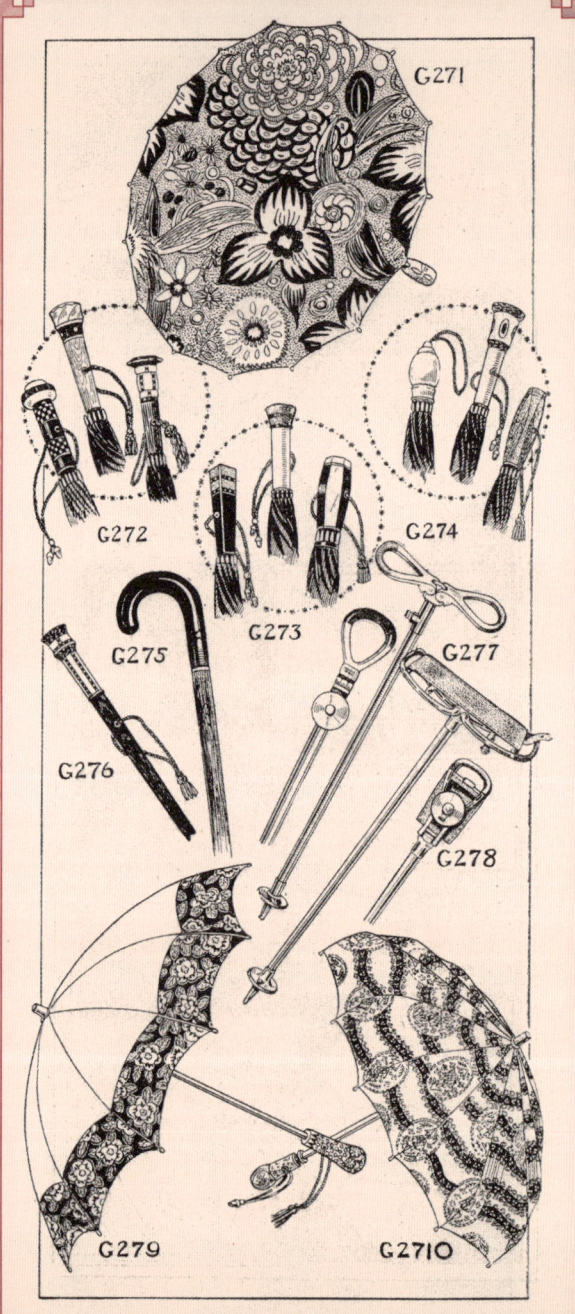

a few days. At the end of that time there will be two quarts of vinegar apparently as strong as the first quart.

SAVE ON CURTAIN POLES.

Broom handles make good curtain poles for the ordinary width door. Chop the stick to fit the width of the door, and paint or enamel to correspond with the furnishings of the room. Supports for the pole can be bought; they are easily adjusted.

SAVE EVEN THE SPROUTS.

A sprouting onion might be thought to be the most hopeless of cases, so far as its usefulness is concerned, but from such an onion there can be grown the finest of young table onions. Not only that, the vegetables can be made exceedingly decorative.

Place four or five of them in a pretty Chinese dish, sprinkle a handful of sand around the roots, add just enough water to cover the bottom of the dish, and stand it in a sunny window. You will discover that to the eye you are growing the aristocratic Chinese lily. The sprouts will shoot up and in about a week you can begin to have young onions to eat and to use in your salads, thus cheating the green-grocer and the garbage-can at one stroke. Cut the sprouts down close to the bulb and they will continue to produce new ones for a long time.

SAVE YOUR UMBRELLA.

Umbrella ribs will not rust and the umbrella consequently will last twice as long if it is placed handle downward when put wet in the umbrella rack—or, better still, if it is allowed to dry while open.

SAVE YOUR HOT-WATER BAG.

Your hot-water bag need not be discarded because of a small hole; cut a strip of adhesive tape to fit, heat it slightly and press it over the hole; it will last quite a long time.

SAVE ON SILK UNDERWEAR.

A silk chemise that has worn out around the top can be made into a nice undervest. Cut off the worn part;

make a new hem with an opening in the middle of the front; run a ribbon through the hem so that the vest can be gathered in on it to make it fit the figure, and attach two ribbon shoulder-straps. Worn silk night-gowns can be cut into chemises in the same way, though these are usually so long, even after cutting off the tops, that some of the bottom must be cut off and a new bottom hem made.

SAVE THE MARRED FURNITURE.

Leather upholstery may be cleaned with any cleansing fluid suitable for leather shoes or gloves of the same color. If the leather does not need cleaning but merely brightening, it may be rubbed with such an oil as paraffin, lemon, neatsfoot or linseed.

The wooden parts of the furniture may have the greasy film removed, which is often present on much-used furniture, by washing it with lukewarm water to which has been added one tablespoonful of kerosene to the pint of water. One part at a time should be washed and rubbed at once with a dry cloth. The furniture may be polished by rubbing with a mixture of two parts boiled linseed-oil and one part of turpentine. This is carefully rubbed into the grain of the wood and the surplus oil removed with a woollen cloth. If the furniture has scratches they may be obscured by applying a small amount of water-color appropriate for wood which matches the color of the furniture. If the scratch is slight a good furniture polish will contain enough dye or stain to cover the scratch.

Scratches on mahogany may be retouched with a permanganate of potash solution in the proportion of one ounce of potassium permanganate crystals to one quart of water.

Boiled linseed-oil, if rubbed in, will darken the wood to some extent.

White spots may be removed from furniture by applying linseed or sweet oil, allowing it to stand for an hour or so, then rubbing vigorously and repeating the process if necessary.

Painted wood should be washed with clear water or soap and water. Whiting applied with a damp cloth will usually remove spots and finger-marks.

SAVE PLUMBING EXPENSE.

An annoyance was experienced recently in having the drain-pipe to the bathroom washbowl become so clogged that water would barely drain out after a long interval. Various remedies were tried, and at last the plumber suggested that often dried-up soap would accumulate in the pipe and that a strong solution of lye would frequently remove it. This was tried with perfect success.

SAVING TAFFETA UNDERSKIRTS.

If taffeta underskirts, when they are new, are first dipped in water and then are hung up to drip until they are dry, they will not split so soon as otherwise.

SAVE THE PEA-PODS.

Many delicious flavors can be imparted to soups by utilizing the bits of vegetables which are usually thrown out. Pea-pods, washed and wrapped in a thin cloth to facilitate taking them from the pot, may be dropped into a broth made from pieces of left-over roast and will give a very distinctive flavor to what would otherwise be rather an insipid dish.

SAVE THE CURTAINS.

The life of a curtain can be lengthened by making the hems on both ends the same width so that either end of the curtain can be put on the pole. Each time the curtain is to be laundered mark the end which was on the pole and, when again hanging it, put the other end on top. In this way the curtain will wear out evenly and so be of use for a longer time.

SAVE THE WASHSTAND.

Is there an old-fashioned washstand with a marble-slab top standing unused in your attic? If so, take off the marble slab and use it in the kitchen for a bread-and-pastry board. Then enamel or paint the stand white or cream color, hang a mirror over it, and you have an attractive dressing table.

SAVE CLIPPINGS.

A very simple file of clippings has proven a veritable friend in need. Store clippings on all sorts of topics in envelopes of ordinary size, say No. 6. Label the envelopes on diagonally opposite corners, so that the label can be at once read, from whichever way the envelope is viewed.

A convenient classification of subjects can be made to suit individual needs and tastes. The envelopes are alphabetically stored in a box.

SAVE ON ENAMEL-WARE.

An enamel pan or saucepan, to which badly burned food sticks, can be made as bright and as good as new if it is soaked in ashes and water for a few hours, then placed in a hot oven and baked until the burned place drops away in the form of ashes.

SAVE VEGETABLE TRIMMINGS.

A soup made on the basis of a few bones is a light vegetable one, in which the green tops of leeks, leaves of celery, stalks of parsley, ends of carrots and the hard heart of a cabbage, diced, are tied in a thin cloth and simmered for about two hours.

SAVE MATTRESSES.

Stick together newspapers enough to entirely cover the springs of your bed, and if there are slats make a second paper sheet to put under the springs. It will keep out the dust and is easily replaced.

SAVE GREASE-MARKED CREPE-DE-CHENE.

Make a thin paste of petrol and French chalk, and coat the stained parts with it thickly. Roll up the dress in a cloth, and leave for several hours. Then take it outside, and shake, and brush off the powder, and leave it in the air till the smell of the petrol disappears.

SAVE THE BROOMS.

There are various ways of either lengthening or shortening the life of a broom. For the usual household purposes select a broom of medium weight with millet that is fine, and light green in color. Have some arrangement for hanging a broom, for it must never stand on the floor brush downward. Two nails just far enough apart to admit the handle of broom just above the brush is an excellent arrangement as the broom slips in and out so easily. Always dip the broom into a pail of warm soapy water once a week to keep it clean and to keep the brush from becoming brittle and breaking at the ends. It is poor economy to work with a worn-out broom. Give it to the men to use in the out-buildings. It can be trimmed even, pretty well back and used for outside scrubbing.

SAVE TAN BOOTS AND SHOES.

After wearing tan boots or shoes for a time they sometimes become dark and discolored. To revive them, mix a tablespoonful of milk with a dessertspoonful of methylated spirit, and apply with a sponge or a piece of flannel, rubbing the leather well. After a few minutes the boots may be cleaned in the usual way.

* * *

QUEER SUPERSTITIONS.

The one who eats the crusts will get all the kisses.

It is unlucky to toast bread on a knife.

You will get a letter if you accidentally drop bread into a cup of tea.

Eat bread that another has bitten and you will quarrel.

If a cake runs over the top of the pan you will get money.

If you burn your bread someone is angry with you.

If your bread falls buttered side down it is a sign that you have committed a sin that day.

If you make good bread you will marry a handsome man.

Household Hints for Wise Women

REFRIGERATION WITHOUT ICE.

In some places where ice is scarce the housewife will find the following suggestion useful: By following a simple scientific process, butter, milk and other foods may be kept at a very low temperature during the hottest weather. An ordinary clay flower-pot or any sort of a clay jar that is not glazed is necessary for the refrigerator temperature. Moisten a cloth with strong salt water and keep it over the flower-pot which covers the dish of food. The ends of the cloth should dip down into a basin in which the flower-pot stands, and in this basin salt water must be kept all the time. The water will circulate through the pores of the pot at such a slow rate of evaporation, that the pot contents are kept cool. The best place for using this simple but valuable principle is near an open window.

A cloth wet with unsalted water will bring the mercury down, but not to the same degree that salt water will accomplish.

WHEN YOU LIE AWAKE.

The woman suffering from insomnia, no matter what the weather, should get a fan and fan continuously for ten or fifteen minutes. The air circulation and the weariness caused by fanning induce prompt slumber.

DANGER FROM AN UNEXPECTED SOURCE.

Never leave a magnifying-glass or a lens of any kind around the home. Often such an article is left on the library table, or in the sewing-basket. A little child found such a magnifying-glass, and the sun's rays condensed through it set fire to its dress and the little one was burned to death. Even a goldfish globe has been known to act as a lens and set fire to a house.

WHEN SEWING.

A very helpful article when sewing is to be done is a pin-cushion fastened to the top part of the machine arm. It is made by winding several thicknesses of flannel around the arm, and fastening same in place with a few stitches. This cushion is always in place and saves much time and bothersome moving about when one is sitting at the machine and needs pins or needles.

MAKE A CLOTHES-PEG BAG.

A convenient clothes-peg bag is made from a square bag just wide enough to have a clothes hanger sewed to the top. A slit is made along the top to within four inches of each end, so that the pegs may be put in and taken out easily.

The advantage of this bag is that it can be hooked on the line, and slid along as the clothes are hung up.

A COLD-WEATHER HINT.

When very cold try this plan: Take at least twenty-five full, deep breaths, holding them as long as possible and letting them out very slowly. This gets up a good circulation so that one is soon warm. For cold feet, use the foot and ankle exercise: While sitting, point the toes downward as far as possible, which strains the muscles over the ankles; then work the feet up and down for at least a dozen times, which will cause a good circulation. If this is done when coming in out of the cold instead of going at once to the fire, much trouble with chilblains will be avoided.

TO MAKE CLOTHES WHITE.

White dresses or underwear that have a bad color should first be soaked in cold water to which a little ammonia has been added and then given a lemon-bleach. That means a large lemon should be cut into slices, and rind and all boiled up in the boiling pot or pan. When at full boiling-point, put in the muslins or linens and boil for twenty minutes.

A QUICK CLEANSER.

To clean porcelain bath-tubs and lavatories quickly and beautifully, the following formula cannot be equalled:

Throw a little coarse salt into the slightly dampened tub, then rub it briskly with a flannel cloth wet with turpentine. The most obstinate stains immediately disappear, leaving the porcelain not only perfectly clean, but also antiseptic, and with a polish superior to that gained by using caustic washing-powders which eventually injure the drain-pipes.

A STOVE HINT.

If you will go over the entire stove while it's slightly warm with a cloth wet with kerosene oil, allow it to dry, then blacken the stove, you will find it will last twice as long and have a polish greater than ever before. Each morning rub it over with an old piece of flannel and see how it will shine.

THAT "BOTHERSOME" DOOR.

How many house-keepers know that when a door "sticks" at the sill or at the top or sides, and the man of the house or neighborhood carpenter is not within call, common yellow soap rubbed on the places will help the trouble and the door will open and shut easily.

TO CLEAN DECANTERS AND GARBAGE CANS

Roll small pieces of blotting-paper into little wads; wet them and soap them well. Put them in the decanters that are one-quarter full with warm (not hot) water; shake them well for a few minutes, then rinse with clear cold water; wipe the outside and stand to drain, and when dry they will be about as bright as new ones.

If a little care is exercised, the life of the humble garbage can may be more than doubled. Each time it is emptied it should be carefully washed with hot soapsuds and then scalded with a solution of sal soda.

If possible it should be sunned for several hours.

A thick lining of newspapers makes the cleaning much more easy, as the garbage does not stick to the sides of the can.

A coat of paint, inside and out, when the can is new will prevent rust.

Also save big paper bags to use inside the can.

IMPROVES THE OVEN.

A coat of whitewash in the inside of an oven saves time and trouble, for it makes the oven easier to keep clean and better for cooking purposes.

DON'T BURN THE HOUSE.

Many fires are caused by accidents in the handling of lanterns. This danger may be greatly reduced by stretching an overhead wire of desirable length in any basement or building where it is necesary to use a portable light. An S-hook, or a harness snap may be hung over the wire to receive the lantern, which may then be moved from one end of the wire to the other as desired.

This will not only reduce the danger of fire to a minumum, but as the light rays fall from above, a larger area will be more efficiently lighted than if the lantern were placed upon the floor.

HANG YOUR SHIRT, TOO.

Wooden dress-hangers can be greatly improved by screwing two small hooks on the under side for skirts. Sew too hoops on each skirt and they will no longer be stretched at the hips or slide off on to the floor.

AN ECONOMICAL IRONING-BOARD COVER

is made from unbleached muslin. Cut the muslin a little larger than the size of the board, hem the edges, and sew tapes about ten inches apart and parallel on the sides of the cloth. These tapes, when tied together under the board, hold on the cover securely. Only one-half the usual amount of material is needed for this covering.

TONIC FOR THE FERNS.

Wet the earth around the ferns every three or four weeks with water in which is a little household ammonia, a teaspoonful to a quart. This refreshes them, and keeps them glossy and green.

TO REMOVE STARCH FROM IRONS.

A piece of door or window screen, folded up where the iron can be rubbed over it occasionally, will help keep starch from irons.

A BUTTONHOLE HINT.

Mark the button-hole with a thread, then work it completely before cutting. In this way you will have a much evener button-hole and it will not ravel. This is especially suited to cotton crepes.

TO CLEAN TARNISHED SILVER

with a minimum amount of labor, make a solution of one teaspoon of cooking soda and one teaspoon of salt to each quart of water in an aluminium kettle. Bring to a boil, lay in the silver and boil until the tarnish disappears. The solution must cover the silver. Plunge silver into a pan of clean boiling hot water and let it stand until cool enough to wash the silver, then rinse in a second pan of hot water.

IN IRONING WOOL OR SILK,

great care should be taken that the iron be not too hot. An iron that is not hot enough to burn may yellow these two fabrics. When a starched garment is yellowed it will usually wash out, as the starch has protected the material.

PEEL ONIONS

while holding them under cold water and the fumes will not reach the eyes and cause them to smart.

WASHING HANDKERCHIEFS

that have been used at the time of heavy colds in the head is often an unpleasant task, but the labor can be lessened by putting the handkerchiefs in a pail of cold water to which one cup of salt has been added, and letting them soak some hours. Without putting the hands into them, work around with the clothes-stick, drain, put through a tepid water, drain and wash as usual.

FELT PADS ON CHAIR LEGS

or any part of furniture that rests on the floor is a great saving of scratches and noise; besides, furniture so protected can be easily moved about. Cut piece of felt to fit, spread with glue, also the place to be covered, and press the pad in place. The weight of furniture makes it very firm. Use pieces of old felt hat.

TO REMOVE A GLASS STOPPER

that is tight in the bottle, wet a cloth in boiling water and wrap it about the neck of bottle. In a short time the stopper is easily removed.

EASE STICKING DRAWERS

by rubbing with hard soap that part which comes in contact with any part of the case. Slightly warmed beeswax is used in the same way.

A HANDFUL OF ASHES

put into a bottle, then half filled with cold water and shaken, will usually remove all stains.

TO WHITEN AND CLEAN A STRAW

or Panama hat, make a paste of sulphur and lemon juice, rub it thoroughly into the straw with an old toothbrush and allow it to dry several hours. Brush off the dry paste with a clean stiff brush.

DO NOT WEEP, BUT WASH.

If your pretty crepe de chine blouse is soiled, do not weep. Here is a way to wash it and at the same time preserve its beauty. Wash in cold water with white soap; rinse thoroughly; if white crepe, add a little bluing to the last rinsing. Hang up to dry. When completely dried, iron without dampening. This preserves the lustre and crepe effect. If the waist has lingerie collar and cuffs, dampen them with a little starch water, or, if you do not care to have them appear stiff, use a little water to which a bit of borax has been added. This will whiten the material as well as give to it the proper stiffness.

STARCH HINTS.

A lump of starch dissolved in water for cleaning windows is more effective than whitening. Boiled starch may be washed over newly cleaned linoleum and allowed to dry. This will form a skin, and if the linoleum is to be polished a very small quantity of polish need be used.

Powdered starch is a good silver polisher, and it is far superior to bread-crumbs, dough, and such like for cleaning soiled wall-paper. Powdered finely and rubbed gently over the walls with a clean, soft duster or an old muslin curtain, it will remove all stains.

A SAUCEPAN HINT.

Here is a simple method of cleaning a saucepan in which milk has been boiled. After pouring out the boiling milk, replace the lid before the steam has time to escape, and allow the saucepan to cool before taking it off again. Then put the pan in cold water to soak. It can be cleaned quickly and easily.

MAKE YOUR OWN SOAP.

Soap-making is a worth-while economy where there is even a very little waste fat each day. The process is very simple. Have ready a five-pound pail of fat that has been melted and cooled to the creamy stage. Dissolve a one-pound can of lye in one quart of cold water, using a good-sized kettle. When cool add one-half cup of cold water in which three teaspoons of borax has been dissolved and one-third cup of household ammonia. Slowly add the fat, continually stirring, and as soon as the mixture is thick and smooth pour it into a baking tin lined with old cloth. Do not stir too long, as it is liable to make the soap granular. Cut into squares before it becomes too hard.

REMOVES WOOD STAINS.

The white mark on any polished wood, that has been caused by placing a hot water jug or anything hot upon it, may be removed by rubbing the place with a little ammonia on a soft piece of flannel.

TO CLEAN CHIFFON.

A good way to clean chiffon is to squeeze it well in warm, soapy water until clean, in which a lump of sugar has been dissolved. This will give a little firmness after being ironed. It is best to dry the chiffon before ironing.

Is Your Judgment Good?

The average man has more and wiser judgment than the average woman. Not because he is a man and she is a woman, but because he has lived more freely amongst men and has seen and weighed the reactions of his course. He has learned by wide and various experience of life. History shows us that from time immemorial women's lives have been more circumscribed than men's. They are only now coming into their inheritance of wider, fuller, more significant living.

Now is the very day for women to stop and reflect; to take careful measurements of their abilities and their wisdom.

I wonder if you know the story of a very typical pagan woman, Medea? Gilbert Murray has of recent years re-translated her story from Euripides, and it sounds quite as if some woman of to-day, some unwise girl, were telling her own story. Medea deceived her father and killed her brother in order to help her lover, Jason. She loved, for the moment indeed, one man more than home, loyalty, truth, gratitude or mercy. It is no wonder then that when her lord tired of her and held up her weaknesses to her, she exclaimed:

"And we who study not our wayfarings
But feel and cry—oh, we are drifting things and evil."

Perhaps that first sentence will give us a clue to one of women's failings. "We who study not our wayfarings." Women can no longer afford to go on as did Medea, feeling, crying and drifting. All stable and true happiness depends upon forethought, judgment, wisdom. Somehow we must grow wiser as we live, for

"We shall not pass this way again."

How then, knowing that life and health and peace and happiness depend upon judgment, how shall we train it?

We can best train our judgment by reflecting carefully upon past actions and their results. Experience must not just sweep us along with it. We must learn to invite and to control experience. There are certain evil things that can happen to us once, but if we are wise and careful, if we are sensible enough to learn by experience, they can never happen again. It is our business to tabulate the results of past actions.

Write down on the tablets of memory or in a little day-by-day book, that such and such actions have reaped such and such results, good or evil. Remember that your chief object in this human life is to establish reliable relationships; to be such a character as others may count upon.

It is even thought, nowadays, as you know, that the conditions of our eternal life may depend upon what success we have in building a character here and now. In this building of character, intellect of course helps, and no-one can justly forego any development of the intellect that is attainable. But remember that judgment is more valuable than intellect.

There is very little deliberate wickedness in the world. Given a certain degree of health and judgment, life would be very livable. Add to it the glow and promise of hope and the sense that this is an eternal adventure we are on, and it becomes a very wonderful and beautiful adventure.

Each day offers us some little turning in the road, and everything depends upon the wisdom with which we choose. We must do all we can to choose sensibly and bear what we must with courage. Then some day, quite unexpectedly, we shall turn and look back on the way we have come and say: "After all, it was success!"

Learn as you go the value of leisure to reflect. Take a few moments every day, not to repine, not to regret what is lost, but to judge your own actions and to choose and invite your future.

If the midnight is upon you, know that the dawn must break. If you are shouldering an unbearable load, know that it must fall or you must fall and wake in another environment, with a new opportunity.

There are no very certain answers, as far as I know, as to whence we have come or where we shall end, but there is a daily choice of wise and unwise action, of haste or reflection; of improvement or a multiplication of mistakes.

Remember in each choice, too, that from your inmost soul will come your stable happiness if it is to come at all. There are people overwhelmed with the goods of this world who are yet utterly wretched. I know of others who are bereft of almost all life's comforts who yet bear every mark of joy on their faces. In your inmost self lies the security which passes accident. Be undisturbed by luck, good or bad. Hold your head high over mischance and bereavement, treachery or failure, and believe that as long as there is life there is a chance to repair and space for judgment to grow and expand.

MY BEST.
C. F.

I've tried to do my best to-day
    As golden hours have sped.
There's little else that I can say
    Now that the day is dead.
I joy to know I've struggled through
    Each pleasure, task, and test.
I've sought to keep a purpose true.
    I've tried to do my best.

I've tried to do my best to-day.
    My best was poor enough.
I may have faltered on the way
    —At times the road was rough.
And now as beams of day depart
    Night brings the peace of rest,
Because in honesty of heart
    I've tried to do my best.

Idle Moments

PARENTS AND CHILDREN.

Parents and children have reciprocal duties and responsibilities throughout life, but that there is variation in the emphasis to be placed upon the duty of care and protection one to the other.

In the early stages of a child's life, unquestionably, the parents' duty is determined by the fact that a child has been given life, not through his own will but through the will of his parents; furthermore to his parents and other forebears he is indebted for his intelligence, the kind of nervous system he has, the kind of body, the kind of predispositions, etc. To them he is likewise indebted for his environment, including education in the home first and foremost; that constant stimulation and moulding which a child breathes in—the home atmosphere which though it involves unconscious tuition the greater part of the time, is nevertheless the most influential in bringing out the best in him and repressing the less desirable. The neighborhood in which a child lives and the school he attends determine largely his choice of associates; the attitude of mind of his parents, whether they care for the things of the spirit or whether their hopes are centred on the things of this world, determine in which direction a child's face is set.

The situations in which obedience is indicated as necessary and right are doubtless not nearly so many as tradition has led us to believe. If an occupation is allowing a natural outlet for a child's activities, we should hesitate to interfere. Furthermore, disobedience, to our adult view, always involves intention.

Look at it from the children's point of view. Outflow of interest, attention and motor expression are not easily checked or diverted on a child's part, so his obedience may be delayed for that reason, or because he may not understand.

If children's disobedience is wilful, isolation from play or playmates or even from the family, often brings home the fact that something is wrong and can only be made right by obedience.

In managing very young children, as well as older ones, it has always been found the surest means of securing instant and absolute obedience is cordial recognition of little acts of helpfulness and obedience.

BEING A FRIEND.

If you can't be a genius, or a field-marshal of big business, or a crowned queen of the social realm, or a wizard of finance, or the admitted leader in one of the learned professions, you can be a friend. If you can't give the rich gifts of tangible things you would like to give, if you can't afford to put at the feet of those you love the best and most beautiful things the world has to offer, you can make the gift of yourself, in the friendly relations of every day, in the circle of the family, in the round of business. The gift is above every other in your bestowal; and it is the gift that you alone can give.

We are only poor if we choose to be, and the poverty that really matters is the poverty of the inner nature, the meagreness and penury of the soul. We all know men and women, distributive blessings, welcome wherever they go, who can give little in the way of things. And sometimes, perhaps, they grieve for it, forgetting that things matter least and that affections, genuine and tender, are what count supremely. They never know the good they do; we cannot tell them. When we need comfort, we seek them out.

Sometimes the medicine we need is most of all to speak out of the overfullness of the mind and heart to a listener whose silence means neither an inattention nor an indifference, but an all-compassing safe harbor and sure refuge in our time of trouble—the shadow of a rock in a weary land, the green oasis, after dusty marching days.

"To be or not to be" a friend—the decision changes life and determines whether our orbit shall be the selfish exclusion of a hermitage or a boundless concern in humanity.

If we deserve friends, we do not want them for the parties they give, the presents they make, the houses they live in; we want them for themselves. It isn't their possessions: it is their hearts we care about.

YOUR CLOTHING.

How much more and warmer clothes do you wear in the winter than in the summer? I fear that many of my readers still pursue the old custom of changing gradually from light cotton to heavy wool. Do you know that some of your sisters do not do this any more and are wearing the same weight underclothes year in and year out. No, they do not suffer with the cold as much as you do with your "heavy winter undies." The reason is simpler than you would suppose. A body that is well protected by heavy outer clothing is stimulated by what little cold fresh air enters the skin pores, and outer garments act as a boiler plate confining the heat which the body throws off. On the other hand, a skin the pores of which are smothered by close contact with some heavy material does not get an honest chance to breathe as it naturally should and the fires of the body-furnace are reduced for lack of proper "draft." A certain amount of cold is stimulating and healthful, otherwise we would not have it. A woman who wears heavy underclothes is uncomfortably warm in a heated house, and when she goes outdoors she feels the cold more readily; one who wears light underclothes is perfectly comfortable in the house, and when she goes out with her heavy coat she has sufficient extra protection against the cold.

FORGET TO HATE.

The most ignoble and dangerous of all human emotions is hatred.

The most futile of all hatreds is that which hugs an injury which is of the past.

The most useless to society is that creature who keeps lugging out fuel to add to this evil flame, all the while squeaking "Lest we forget, lest we forget."

The wise, sane woman is she whose whisper of warning is: "Lest we do not forget."

IS THERE A SANTA CLAUS?

A little girl once wrote Charles A. Dana, a great editor, inquiring if there is a Santa Claus. She said her little friends denied his existence. Dana's answer is preserved in many scrap-books. It follows:

"Virginia, your little friends are wrong. They have been affected by the scepticism of a sceptical age. They do not believe except they see. They think that nothing can be which is not comprehensible to their little minds. All minds, Virginia, whether they be men's or children's, are little. In this great universe of ours man is a mere insect, an ant, in his intellect, as compared with the boundless world about him, as measured by the intelligence capable of grasping the whole of truth and knowledge.

"Yes, Virginia, there is a Santa Claus. He exists as certainly as love and generosity and devotion exist, and you know that they abound and give to your life its highest beauty and joy. Alas! how dreary would be the world if there were no Santa Claus. It would be as dreary as if there were no Virginias. There would be no child-like faith then, no poetry, no romance, to make tolerable this existence. We should have no enjoyment except in sense and sight. The eternal light with which childhood fills the world would be extinguished.

"Not believe in Santa Claus? You might as well not believe in fairies! You might get your papa to hire men to watch in all the chimneys on Christmas eve to catch

Santa Claus, but that is no sign that there is no Santa Claus. The most real things in the world are those that neither children nor men can see. Did you ever see fairies dancing on the lawn? Of course not; but that's no proof that they are not there.

"Nobody can conceive or imagine all the wonders there are unseen and unseeable in the world. You may tear apart the baby's rattle and see what makes the noise inside, but there is a veil covering the unseen world which not the strongest man, nor even the united strength of all the strongest men that ever lived, could tear apart. Only faith, fancy, poetry, love, romance, can push aside that curtain and view and picture the supernal beauty and glory beyond. Is it real? Ah, Virginia, in all this world there is nothing else real and abiding. No Santa Claus? Thank God! he lives and he lives for ever. A thousand years from now, Virginia, nay, ten times ten thousand years from now, he will continue to make glad the heart of childhood."

WORDS FITLY SPOKEN.

Keep the heart lights brightly burning; keep the heart fires flaming with joy and courage and inspiration. Remember that lovingly spoken, sympathising words are the best kind of kindlings for the heart fires. The fire they light in the morning does not need making over again the whole day long, for it keeps coals over night, a good warm, glowing bed, all ready for the next day. Who does not know the comfort of opening the ashes on the hearth on a winter morning and finding a cheery bed of coals to begin the day with? That is the way a kind, loving word lasts. The pressure of duties and the hurry of things may seem to have obliterated it, but the breath of memory soon fans it into life again and makes life happier, brighter, more worth living.

Why do we not speak such words oftener? Why do we not remember to praise those who have tried to please us, to whom a kind, grateful, appreciated word would be like a tonic to the soul? Why do we not to our nearest and dearest speak words of affection, assurances of love, say oftener in so many words what they already know, but which the loving heart never tires of hearing over and over again.

AVOIDING AN UNHAPPY MARRIAGE.

I will venture that 50 per cent. of unhappy marriages are caused by lack of understanding respecting the duties and obligations of the marriage contract before it is assumed. It has always seemed strange to me that people use so little judgment in taking such an important step. I don't believe that you can reduce so sacred a thing as marriage to business principles any more than you can the practice of religion, but I do believe that many incompatible marriages and much unhappiness could be avoided if young people would sit down and talk things over with the view of coming to a clear notion as to just how each understands the marriage contract before it is entered into.

They ought to realize just what marriage is going to mean to them, just about what each expects of the other and just what compromises and sacrifices each will have to make. In plain words it is well to temper your mutual love with a little mutual common sense. Unfortunately marriage is not always the continual romance that young people are looking for, but it will come a great deal closer to the ideal if wisdom and foresight are mingled with affection. How are you going to manage your home? Who is going to have the final "say-so" regarding purely domestic matters? These and dozens of other questions might well be answered before the final contract is made. This is not commercializing marriage. Such practice would destroy none of the romance and might prevent much unhappiness later.

MOVING AWAY.

To live many years in one place, to know everybody and then to move away—how many of us have had that experience and the equally hard one of trying to settle down in a strange town, make new friends, find a new church and weave new ties. It can be done, but it is not easy. It takes some women longer to become acclimated than others. One of the hardest things I know of is to move away from the old home town—perhaps the very place where you were born and grew up. Almost every niche and corner of the place is endeared to you. And when you move away the old scenes are missed. Parting brings home-sickness, of course. Perhaps you will even take the home paper to keep track of the news from the old place. It is not so easy for a woman to settle down to the daily routine of living in a new locality.

THE NEW LANGUAGE THAT IS OURS

We usually think of the English we speak as a language long established. Yet words that seem as familiar to us as breathing were unknown a comparatively short time ago, just as the civilizations of Egypt and Greece, which we are accustomed to regard as ancient, are really but of yesterday when their two or three thousand years of age are compared with the rude beginnings of man five hundred thousand years ago. Most people, for instance, probably think that the word "starvation" is as old as the language; but it isn't. It was first used—think of it! —in 1775 in a speech made in Parliament by Henry Dundas, who in consequence became widely known as Starvation Dundas.

"Intensify" and "outsider" are two words less than a hundred years old. The English poet, Coleridge, deliberately coined the former word because there was no other in existence to express the particular shade of meaning which he wished to convey.

Other words unknown until the middle of the seventeenth century include such now-familiar ones as "sculptor," "umbrella," "opera," "suicide" and "peninsula," while Bentley in the eighteenth century had actually to defend himself for using such strange terms as "timid," "concede," "repudiate," "idiom" and "vernacular," and George Campbell in 1776 hesitated to use such queer new words as "originate," "sentimental" and "criminality."

"CATTINESS."

Of all the ugly things which creep into the human soul and distort the charm of a woman I believe that "cattiness" is the most poisonous. Cattiness is only another name for a certain kind of envy and jealousy. The catty woman carries about an habitual sneer, an ugly droop of the corner of her mouth and a cynical curl of her lip. Besides spoiling her own life she is a constant trouble maker for others. You know the type! You have heard her purr out her subtle envy under the cloak of kindness. She makes the apparently casual remark: "It's too bad about those Nelson girls. They're the dearest things. I wonder that neither of them has ever had a real beau." She says this out of jealousy, because she knows that the Nelson girls are nice looking and that they get more attention than she does.

A little later in life you still see her at work. She congratulates the new minister on his appointment of Mrs. Smith as chairman of the social committee. "I think we ought to all pitch in and help her," she purrs in the unsuspecting minister's ear. "If for no other reason, just to show her that we like her in spite of the awful things which have been said about her." Mrs. Cat knows that nothing awful has been said about Mrs. Smith. She merely wants a chance to spread her poisonous envy because her rival was preferred to her. Her experience in neighborhood gossip has taught her that the minister will want to know all about the charges made against Mrs. Smith and from that time on he can't help but think less of the woman whom he thought almost perfect a few minutes before. If you have any cat tendencies cropping out, kill them at once, even if they have nine lives.

"SETTLING DOWN."

After the wedding day come the amazing experiences of the newly-wedded couple who "settle down" to keep house. As might be expected, the majority of mistakes made by the brides (those game enough to 'fess up) are along cooking lines—the rice that swelled and swelled and swelled, originally intended for one pudding; the mistake of buying 2/- worth of soup-greens; also the layer-cake that by some mysterious process rose to heights unknown in the oven and became a gigantic mountain peak, to the anguish and tearful gaze of the young cook. A brand new wife told me that she went to look for the dish-rag after cooking some spinach but couldn't find it. Hubby enjoyed the spinach immensely until the missing sink article was found in the bottom of the dish, stained a green color. Next day the bride wrapped the green cloth up in paper and "lost" it two streets from home. The husband never cared for spinach after that; he liked eggs better—so easy to cook, he explained. Queer, wasn't it! I also knew of two brides who gave their maiden names when purchasing groceries after marriage. Sounds funny, doesn't it? But all women have similar experiences to laugh over, and some husbands laugh with their wives, not "at" them.

USE BRITISH PERFUME.

What kind of perfume do you use? Do you take care to select only those odors that blend with your personality? What is best for one woman may not be so good for another; the perfume a woman uses should be as pleasing to the senses as her character and physical charm. But it should be used sparingly! Too much perfume is worse than none at all; only a lingering fragrance should reach the nostrils. Many woman think that only foreign perfumes are worth serious classification and that British perfumes are "all alike." This is a mistaken idea; the made-in-the-Empire product is as good as the best anywhere. British perfume houses search the world over for the finest flower essences, rare spices and precious oils, to be blended into perfumes. And there is an English perfume to suit your own individual self.

* * *

Those who are close with money are very often liberal with advice.

* * *

The man who cannot be caught with whiskey may be ruined with money.

* * *

Some of the hungriest men in the world to-day are those who have the most wealth.

A 3411—Luce's Eau-de-Cologne, 2/6 Bottle

A 3410—Atkinson's Eau-de-Cologne, Wicker Bottles, 3/11 and 6/11

A 3412—Luce's Green Bottle Lavender and Musk, or Eau-de-Cologne, 1/- Bottle

Items of Interest to Every Woman

When a baby is 1 year old it should have 6 teeth; at 1½, 12 teeth; at 2, 16 teeth and at 2½ years, 20 teeth—if the baby is normal.

* * *

To find out whether a girl loves him, says a wise writer, let a young man refer to some trifling detail of the previous conversation. Something very trivial, it must be. If she remembers, let him go to the nearest jeweler.

* * *

It is a curious fact, if you will look around, that a boy under 15 is, generally speaking. handsomer than a girl. The reason for this is that the boy's form is more like that of the mature woman than that of the girl. But between 18 and 25 the case is reversed and the girl is more beautiful than the young man. Then once more the contrast is reversed and a man between 40 and 60 is apt to be more handsome than a woman, for the average woman by the neglect of the laws of health and exercise becomes earlier too rotund or too angular, while the man, with exercise, keeps himself "fit."

* * *

Tell a woman, casually as it were, says an authority on the fair sex, of the effect of her beauty or intelligence on a third party, and it will win her to you more than a bushel of your own best compliments.

* * *

Give a girl a chance to say one bright thing to you, and comment on it, says a writer, and she will love you more than if you had said a hundred bright things to her.

* * *

For a woman to be physically perfect she should measure as follows: Height, 63 inches; breadth of neck,

4 inches, breadth of shoulders, 16 inches; waist, 9½ inches; hips, 13 inches. These are the measurements of the Venus de Medici, "the statue that enchants the world," and represents to all artists the perfect type of female form.

* * *

What becomes of the millions of pins? is a question that never seems settled. But one man gave a good and reasonable solution of the mystery: "A surface ten miles square contains nearly 310,000,000 square yards. Assume this as the area of any large city. To include the area of floor surface in houses, it may safely be trebled—say 1,000,000,000 square yards. If every five square yards contained one stray pin, who would be aware of it? Here, then, we have in any large city alone a receptacle for 200,000,000 stray pins unperceived by anybody. The answer, therefore, is that thousands of millions of lost pins can be, and are, scattered about the land unnoticed. Half of these, being outdoors, are gradually destroyed by rust; the other half pass outdoors by degrees."

* * *

A man adds five years to his life if he marries; a woman, four. Those are the latest figures. A busy student has taken 100,000 cases and tried to find out if marriage shortens or lengthens life. Here are the results, with the same true of woman:

Deaths

	Married	Unmarried
From 20 to 25 years	597	1,174
From 25 to 30 years	865	1,369
From 30 to 35 years	907	1,475
From 40 to 45 years	1,248	1,689
From 60 to 65 years	3,385	4,330
From 65 to 70 years	8,055	10,143
From 80 to 85 years	17,400	19,688

Is Your Child Comfortable?

NAUGHTINESS IS FREQUENTLY CAUSED BY DISCOMFORT.

The other day I chanced to be visiting in a home where there is a lovely little child of about three years. It was a hot and humid day. The child fretted, cried and was obviously unhappy. The mother scolded and even spanked with no effect.

"I know he isn't hungry," she said despairingly, "and he can't be sleepy." It was hardly noon. "He isn't sick, he's just plain cross."

Being an old friend of the family, the mother asked if I would look after little Tommy while she went on an errand. I was glad to do it for I wanted to try an experiment. I took the child to the bath-room and undressed him. He had on rompers with long sleeves, a waist, shirt, stockings and shoes. The straps of his waist were too long and slipped down over his arm. If there is any one thing more than another that will make me want to cry—or worse!—on a hot, sweaty day, it is to have a shoulder strap slip down over my arm. The grip to a garter was worn out, so one stocking hung by only one garter and the elastic was out of this. At every step that stocking slewed around and pulled. His shirt was woollen and too heavy. Someone had told the mother not to take off woollen shirts until he was four years old, so, hot or cold, she left on a woollen shirt. His rompers were too small and drew in the crutch. A saint would have been "cross," wearing those clothes.

I took off all the child's garments, put him in the tub and let him stay there while I did some repairing. The straps to the waist were shortened. The band was taken off the rompers and a piece stitched on to make them longer in the seat.

When Tommy was taken out of the tub and dried, I sprinkled talcum powder generously over back and chest where the prickly shirt had irritated the tender flesh. A thinner shirt of silk and wool was substituted for the woollen, with later advice to the mother to change this to cotton. A healthy child of three years doesn't need a woollen shirt in hot weather any more than a cat needs an overcoat. Socks were put on instead of stockings and the sleeves of the rompers were cut off above the elbow and hemmed.

When Tommy was dressed, he had a drink of cool fruit juice and went kicking his joyous little heels into the yard to play. The transformation had taken exactly half an hour.

After his mother had been home a few moments, she remarked on how happily Tommy seemed to be playing and wondered what had occasioned the change. I told her. He was simply made comfortable.

"I just didn't think," she said, "that he might not be comfortable."

A normal child is not cross unless he has reason to be and that reason may be either sickness or discomfort—discomfort oftener than sickness.

A baby wearing nappies is most uncomfortable unless the nappy is carefully adjusted. With young girls sometimes taking care of the baby and with the mother hurriedly changing the nappy many times a day, carelessness often brings great discomfort and consequent irritability. If the nappy is pinned to the shirt, there is danger of dragging the shirt down on the neck until the neckband of the shirt positively hurts. If it is not pinned in the back, it will slip down and bind the legs.

Usually a smaller nappy or pad is worn inside the square and unless this is pinned up front and back, it slips down into a bunch between the legs. I have seen a baby waddling about like a little duck with a great wet pad of nappy between his legs. The rubber pants are good to use in necessity but are too often the device of a lazy nurse or mother to protect outer garments and leave inner ones wet.

The little rompers may very easily be too small and although they can be buttoned on over the nappy, it is done only by bunching the nappy up and restricting the freedom of the legs. It is such restriction and irritation of delicate parts of the body that often engender bad habits.

The nappy should be loose and comfortable, not too thick and both outer and inner cloth pinned securely front and back. And, better yet, the child taught to go without a nappy as early as possible.

Stockings pulling on the legs or wrinkling down over the shoes are uncomfortable. Shoes must be plenty large and with firm but not too heavy soles. Rubber nappies should not be so small in the leg that they leave a red mark. And they should not be worn except when absolutely necessary.

In dressing a child, remember his comfort as well as his looks. The day of starched, embroidered, white picture dresses is about gone by, thank heaven. The colored rompers and little gingham romper suits are so attractive that even the vainest mother is willing to have her child wear clothes in which he can play. Children used to be so fearfully "dressed up" on Sundays, afternoons and visiting days that they had to be set upon a chair to be looked at, or decide between stealing off for a good time with certain punishment to follow, and miserable, unhappy, immaculate doing nothing. Invariably the wisdom of child nature chose the former.

Do not forget to give the child too small to ask for it, frequent drinks of water. I have seen a child's frettings instantly stopped by a drink of cold water. Little children get just as thirsty as big ones or grown folks, and yet we "forget" to give them a drink and scold them when they cry for it. And the body needs water. Thirst is Nature's warning and should be heeded. Babies and dogs often suffer by thirst just because those who are responsible for them forget to give them a drink.

In summer, keep the children out of doors pretty much all of the time, and in winter as much as possible. When they sleep see that their rooms are of comfortable temperature, neither too hot nor too cold. A child is often fretful and wakeful simply because his room is too hot. Let the covering be ample but light.

If the skin shows rash in hot weather, use carbolated vaseline after cleansing with warm water and pure castile soap. A good healing talcum powder after the bath, even if there is no rash, is comforting.

If there is severe chafing after bowel trouble, use zinc ointment. The effect is magical. In winter when the skin gets rough, use healing cold cream, mentholatum or honey and almond cream.

Do not put coarse wool or heavy fleece-lined underwear on children. Many a child has developed seriously wrong habits on account of irritations produced by rough underwear. Sacrifice elsewhere to give them soft underwear that will not scratch or irritate. School rooms are often so illy ventilated that children suffer from too heavy clothing. They get dull and then the teacher scolds. Put more outer wraps on and dress them so they will be comfortable indoors.

The mental development depends greatly on the physical well-being. If a child is well and comfortable he is disposed toward goodness. The mental, moral and spiritual training should begin in infancy but unless a baby's body is healthy and feels comfortable, his mind is not in a condition to receive training.

A good rule for conversations; never say anything that anyone might wish unsaid.

* * *

Have you visited the school this year? Your interest belongs there if you believe in your community.

* * *

Only the real friends travel the uphill roads with you.

* * *

The attitude of a nation toward child welfare will soon become the test of its civilization.—Herbert Hoover.

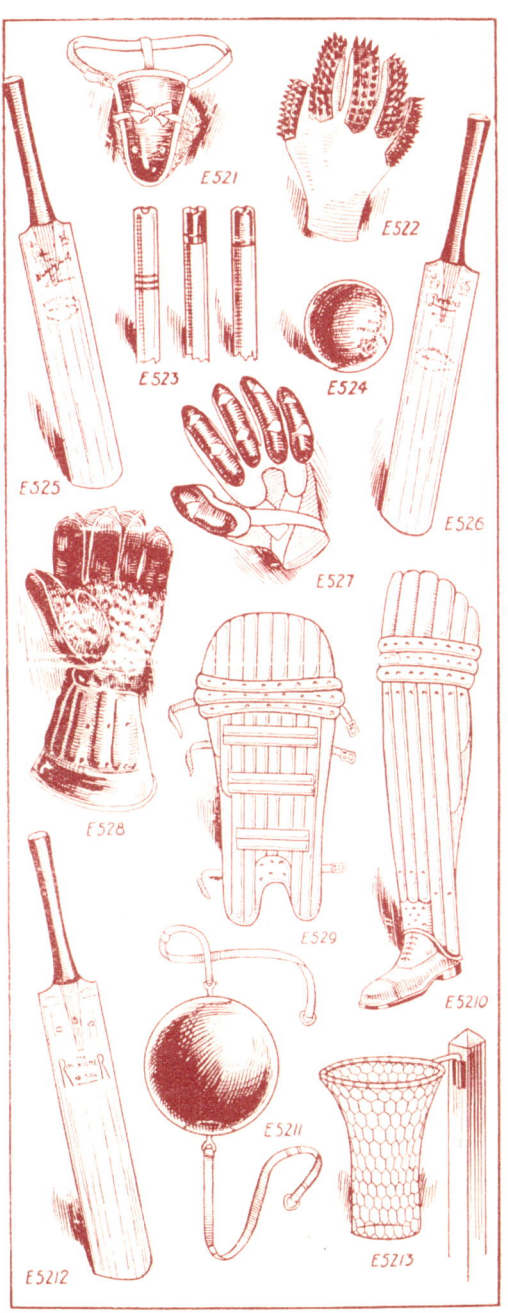

Hints for Beauty

A SERIES OF DON'TS.

Don't tolerate the so-called "lazy" nose. It is the duty of this organ to inhale fresh air and carry it to the lungs. See that it performs this duty, and you may help it by keeping the nose free from dust and all obstructions.

Don't sleep with the head high. If possible, lie perfectly flat upon the bed, or at least with but a flat pillow under the head. Hold the chin high, however, and keep the facial muscles tense to prevent their sagging.

Don't forget that the parched face relishes a drink of cool water quite as much as the parched throat. Fill a bowl with cool, soft water and, holding the breath, immerse the face several times in it. You will be surprised at the result.

Don't dress by a poor light. Have your dressing-table placed where it will receive a good, evenly distributed light at all times.

Don't try to remove the wax from the ears. Doctors advise that this may prove injurious, and if left alone, the wax will form in small balls and drop out of its own accord.

Don't entrust the massage of your face to an amateur. Bad massage is worse than none, and the amateur may cause wrinkles rather than eliminate them. The masseur should receive proper instruction to understand thoroughly the muscles of the face.

Don't dry the hair by artificial heat when you may use the warm, healing rays of the sun. The artificial modes of drying tend to make the hair brittle, while the sun imparts new life to the hair.

Don't try to reduce the weight too quickly. Remember that nature must be given a chance to readjust itself to new conditions, and if not given this chance, more harm than good may result.

Don't forget to smile. It will soon become a habit, and one of the best habits on can form, for every woman looks better smiling, and one cannot think wrinkle-forming thoughts with a smile on the face.

Don't despair of the ageing neck. Feed it carefully with a good cold cream and hold the head high. Give it the same attention that you give your face, and it will in time regain its appearance of youth.

Don't imagine for one moment that beauty will take care of itself. Care must be exercised to retain that which we have, and more care must be taken to attain that which is within our reach. Were it easy of attainment, beauty would be of far less value, and yet too few women realize how willing nature is to assist us.

Don't overtax the stomach, by pouring into it any and every kind of food and drink. Upon this organ depends much of our bodily health which in turn determines to a great extent our foundation for beauty. Treat the stomach kindly, and it will reciprocate in kindness by aiding both health and beauty.

Don't massage the soft skin directly below the eyes. It will cause wrinkles. Better to use a mild astringent, care being taken not to get it in the eye.

Don't lie down or sit down immediately after eating. Stand or walk slowly for at least twenty minutes.

Don't bite your nails. This habit will cause them to become coarse and broad. Biting the cuticle is even worse. Avoid these nervous traits, and remember that proper care of the hands and nails is as essential as proper care of the face.

Don'ts for bathing. There are two things that one with a delicate skin should remember when taking a bath. Be careful not to use too much hot water as it unduly relaxes the facial muscles. Do not overdo the use of a towel in drying oneself. Pat the skin with the towel and fan it.

BLEACHING THE SKIN.

Sulphur vapor baths are recommended for bleaching the skin, and the process may be assisted by an internal use of sulphur. This may be taken in molasses or in boiled milk, using two teaspoonfuls of sulphur to a teacupful of milk an hour before breakfast. Much is claimed for the virtues of sulphur as a clarifier of the blood, and, as everybody knows, good blood is absolutely necessary for a good complexion.

TRIM ANKLES.

To develop the legs, place a book, one or two inches thick, upon the floor. Place your heel upon the floor and the ball of your foot upon the book and lift the entire weight of your body until you are standing upon the book. Gradually let your weight down until your heel touches the floor again. Do this ten times with each foot, then with both feet. As your ankles become accustomed to the strain, choose a thicker book and raise your weight upon that. This will develop the calves of the leg and will make the ankles trim.

CONCERNING THE MOUTH.

If you would have a pretty mouth, avoid biting the lips. It is not a good plan to moisten the lips often with the tongue, for it not only tends to discolor and dry them but also will cause them to chap.

If the lips are too thick, the mouth should be frequently moistened with an astringent lotion.

Exceedingly thin lips should be bathed with stimulating lotions and the mouth should not be kept habitually closed or the lips compressed.

Temperamental, impulsive women, fond of ease and pleasure, with cold and fickle natures, are sure to have full, red, pouting lips.

When lips curve upwards, with a slight pout, they usually signify a character whose experience in life has been very small and whose sympathies have never been developed.

Lips curving downward when in repose may mean a sorrowing nature.

PRESERVE YOUTH.

Sitting up late at night will cause grey hair as will nothing else. It makes those dark circles about the eyes, and causes the "windows of the soul" to lose half their luster and softness and beauty. Who ever saw a pretty woman with dull, lifeless eyes? She wouldn't be pretty were she so afflicted. By sleeping properly, the body is kept stronger and fresher, and thus the complexion is benefited greatly. Wrinkles do not come so soon, the skin does not take on that muddy yellow hue as it would otherwise, and cheeks are pink and rosy with that greatest of all rouges—health.

CARE OF THE HANDS.

Keep your hands pliant by making your hands tense and then opening and closing the fingers with the arms extended before you.

Dry the hands thoroughly after a bath.

Keep your hands and nails clean above all else.

And manicure your nails once every twenty-four hours!

ONIONS FOR BEAUTY.

Nothing is so good for the complexion as fresh fruit and vegetables.

Oranges and apples are good for clearing the blood; so are cress and celery. Fruit has the best effect if eaten first thing in the morning.

The finest vegetable to eat if you want a nice complexion is the onion, which contains surphur and also has a laxative tendency.

Spinach and tomatoes contain iron, and should bring color to the pallid cheek. Cabbage purifies the blood, as do the other green vegetables and acid fruits.

There is nothing to touch the lemon, the juices of which can be taken in any form, as another fine complexion improver. Hot lemonade, sipped just before going to bed, is a splendid cure for sleeplessness. If taken cold and strong in the morning it will brighten your eyes, and cure constipation.

The use of drugs and cosmetics will never give you a clear skin; you can only obtain this by keeping in perfect health, and the eating of plenty of fresh fruit and vegetables will help you to this end.

Remember, however, that it is no use eating those fruits that disagree with you, for what suits one person may not suit another. One man's meat may be another man's poison.

UNSIGHTLY PIMPLES.

Girls who are troubled with pimples should get rid of them. That they are unsightly is reason enough for seeking a remedy. A person with a pimpled face should not massage it. Use very hot towels and then open the pimples with a needle that has been sterilized by holding the point in a flame for a few seconds and dipping it into hydrogen peroxide. The matter from the pimples should be gently pressed out and even some of the first blood drawn. Watch the diet closely, avoiding fresh breads and pastry, highly seasoned foods, too much candy or too much meat. Eat plain food and plenty of fresh fruit and vegetables. If these precautions fail, see a doctor.

CARE OF THE EYES.

Though our sight is one of the most precious senses we possess, how very little real care we take of it!

Who is there that does not read while travelling by train? The vibration is very harmful to the eyes if they are made to work; so let them rest in the train, and save your sight for reading at home.

It is a great mistake to read by firelight. It is far too unsteady a light and causes undue strain on the eyes.

A dim light means eye-strain, so does reading in bed, especially if you have only a candle to see by. Though reading in bed may help you to go to sleep, it is bound to affect your sight eventually if you practice it regularly.

Staring at bright lights is another fruitful source of trouble. You have only to look at the sun for a moment or two, as you know, to be blinded temporarily. Do this frequently, and a permanent disability will result.

People who overfeed, or take their meals irregular, are asking for eye trouble later on; so are those who sit about with damp feet—the cold they think they're in for is only one of the minor evils to which they are liable.

The best position for reading is to hold the body erect and let the light come over the left shoulder, if possible. If you use your eyes much with the head bent, or leaning forward, too great a quantity of blood will flow to the eyes, and they will begin to ache.

Place your bed with the head towards the window, then you won't have to stare at the light when you wake.

* * *

KEEP YOUNG.

Next to food there is nothing we need so much as fresh air and the more of it we get the better. Always sleep in a room that is filled with fresh air. Keep your windows open wide all night, even in winter. I have friends who are afraid of fresh air and their complexion which invariably is sallow shows it. With women it is all-important to have a good color and a natural color is infinitely better than an artificial one. Even though she might look the same (which is hardly possible) a woman who relies on cosmetics to give her that "bloom of youth" is merely deceiving herself as to her physical condition. Fresh air will do more for a woman's complexion than all the cosmetics ever manufactured, to say nothing of the greater thing—good health.

* * *

A bachelor between 30 and 50 stands more than twice the chance of passing away that a married man does; 31 out of every thousand bachelors pass away between those ages, and only 14 married men. With women the difference is not so great: 17 out of every thousand single women pass away and 14 married women. But in every case, from 20 to 80 the chances for life favor the married men and married women.

Cooking Hints

USES FOR PINEAPPLES SKINS.

Wash the pineapple before paring, then chop or cut the pineapple skins into small pieces; put into a saucepan with four cupful of cold water and a few grains of salt and let stand for several hours; boil slowly for two hours; press through a strainer, then strain through a piece of cheesecloth or muslin, and to each cupful of strained stock add three-quarters of a cupful of sugar. This syrup is used in fruit tapioca pudding, gelatin or sauce for pudding; one cupful of sugar to each cupful of stock, and a little lemon juice, makes a good syrup to serve with waffles, hot cakes, boiled rice or cereals.

USES FOR ORANGE AND LEMON PEEL.

Every household has oranges and lemons some time during the year. Instead of throwing away the rinds use them as follows: Cover the orange or lemon peel with cold water, adding two tablespoonfuls of salt to a quart of water. Put in a cold place for twenty-four hours; drain, then cover with boiling water; boil slowly for one hour; drain, cut into thin slices and spread on a plate to dry; then boil one cupful of sugar with one cupful of water for three minutes; add the skins and boil for fifteen minutes; remove the syrup; spread on a platter or plate and sprinkle with granulated sugar; dry either in the hot sun or in a cool oven. Pack in a glass jar or pasteboard box for winter use.

TURN YOUR DRIPPINGS INTO FAT.

Put two cupfuls of any fat into a pot; add two quarts of cold water, put over a slow fire and bring to the boiling point; add two cupfuls of raw potato parings and half a cupful of crushed eggshells; boil for two hours, and add water if needed. There must be two quarts at end of two hours; strain through a colander into a shallow pan and set aside until hard. Remove and put the fat into an iron frying pan in the oven until all the water has evaporated; strain through cheese-cloth into a crock or kettle.

FOR THE THRIFTY COOK.

Small left-over portions of fish may be freed from bone and creamed, used with suitable vegetables as a salad, or made into fish croquettes.

Unsightly left-over portions of fowl may be freed from bone, chopped up with the dressing, moistened with any remaining gravy, and made into a loaf or small patties. A little dried, crumbled bread may be added if necessary.

Small left-over portions of white cereals such as cream of wheat and oatmeal, may be moulded in small, individual dishes with a little fruit such as cherry or peach in the bottom. These with cream are good for dessert or for a breakfast dish.

A very little left-over, cold boiled ham may be chopped and used as a filling for an omelette before folding.

Left-over cake may be crumbled, laid in alternating layers with fresh or canned fruit in a buttered baking dish, and a custard mixture of one pint of milk, two eggs, a pinch of salt, a seasoning of cinnamon and three tablespoonfuls of sugar poured over. Bake until nicely set. Or the cake may be cut into dice and a boiled custard turned over, the whites of the eggs being used as a meringue. In this case, season with vanilla in place of cinnamon, and serve very cold.

A small portion of chicken meat of which there is insufficient to serve, may be heated in a cream sauce and a pint of large fat oysters added. Prepare the oysters by removing the tough muscle and washing to free of sand and bits of shell. Season the cream sauce nicely and serve with freshly boiled rice. Make a little mound of the rice on the plate with a dent in the top. Finish with chicken and oysters. Or the chicken and oyster mixture may be served on warm baking powder biscuit freshly baked and broken open.

VEGETABLE PARASITES.

Before using green vegetables of any kind, turn the heads down in salted water to which a few teaspoonsful of vinegar have been added. If this is done, all forms of animal life will crawl out.

CRUSHED EGG-SHELLS.

Eggshells are used to clarify a clear soup. It is well to dry the eggs-shells and put them into a jar; then when egg-shells are needed and you have no fresh egg-shells on hand the jar of dried ones will be handy. Egg-shells are also useful in clarifying fat drippings and coffee.

HOW TO SLICE A PINEAPPLE.

The toughness of pineapples is almost wholly eliminated by slicing the fruit up and down, from stem to blossom end, instead of through the core as is usually done. Thrust a fork into the blossom end to hold the apple steady, and slice until you come to the hard pithy core, which you can then discard.

This way of slicing makes all the difference in the world in the tenderness of the fruit which is usually hard and chippy when sliced with, instead of against the grain.

PREPARING SUET.

In removing the skin from suet a good deal is wasted, but if it is prepared in the following way none is lost. Purchase one or two pounds of beef suet, put it in a stewpan, and place it on the stove where it will melt very gradually without boiling. When it has melted, strain it into a bowl, and it will keep good for weeks.

TO PRESERVE EGGS TO KEEP FOR TWELVE MONTHS.

Put into an earthenware pan two lumps of unslacked lime, about the size of the hand, pour on by degrees two gallons of boiling water. While this is being done the water will make a slight explosive noise; wait until it ceases, and by degrees add the remainder of the water. Leave the lime-water until the next day, stir it up with a stick, drop the eggs in one by one gently, and cover the pan over either with its own lid or a piece of board. The eggs should be put into the lime within four days of being laid, and can be added until the pan is full. Stir up the lime with the hand occasionally (there is no fear of hurting the skin), this prevents the eggs at the bottom getting embedded. Take care that the shells of the eggs are perfect, and if the liquid in the pan evaporates, add from time to time a little cold water, so the eggs are always covered.

MEASURES AND WEIGHTS.

Four teaspoonfuls equal one tablespoonful (liquid).
Four tablespoonfuls equal one wineglassful or half a gill.
Two wineglassfuls equal to one gill, or half a cup.
Two gills equal one coffeecupful, or sixteen tablespoonfuls.
Two coffeecupfuls equal one pint.
Two pints equal one quart.
Four quarts equal one gallon.
Two tablespoonfuls equal one ounce (liquid).
One tablespoonful of salt equals one ounce.
Sixteen ounces equal one pound, or a pint of liquid.
Four coffeecupfuls of sifted flour equal one pound.
One quart of unsifted flour equals one pound.
Eight or ten ordinary-sized eggs equal to one pound.
One pint of sugar equals one pound white granulated.
Two coffeecupfuls of powdered sugar equal one pound.
One coffeecupful of cold butter, pressed down, equals half a pound.
One tablespoonful of soft butter, well-rounded, equals one ounce.
An ordinary tumberful equals one coffeecupful, or half a pint.
About twenty-five drops of any thin liquid will fill a common-sized teaspoon.
One pint of finely-chopped meat, packed solidly, equals one pound.

Tested Recipes

TOMATO SOUP.

Two lb. of tomatoes, 2 oz. of bacon, 1 oz. of dripping, 1 oz. of sago, 1 carrot, 1 onion, 1 stick of celery, 1 qrt. of stock, a bunch of parsley and herbs, salt and pepper. Cut the bacon into small bits, and fry it in the dripping for a few minutes. Wash and prepare the vegetables and cut them up into small dice; fry them in the dripping for about ten minutes; next slice and add the tomatoes, add also the stock and herbs. Put the lid on the pan, and cook the contents till they are tender, then rub them all through a sieve; put the soup back into the pan, bring it to the boil, then sprinkle in the sago. Let the soup boil till the sago is quite clear. Season the soup nicely with salt, pepper, and a dust of caster sugar.

MOCK TURTLE SOUP.

Clean and split an ox foot, and take two onions with their skins on to darken the soup, a few cloves, one tablespoonful of vinegar, peppercorns, and salt to taste, a little celery seed and carrots, and a small piece of turnip. Simmer gently for about six hours, strain through a sieve, then mix two tablespoonfuls of arrowroot, add a glass of sherry, let it boil, carefully stirring, add some forcemeat balls and serve. FORCEMEAT BALLS.—Take 1 teaspoonful of sage, pepper, and salt, 1 egg slightly beaten, $\frac{1}{4}$ lb. of lean bacon or pork, a few breadcrumbs, mixed all together; the bacon to be finely minced; shape all into balls the size of marbles, and fry in boiling lard until a light brown.

MILK AND EGG SOUP.

One quart of milk, 2 eggs, $\frac{1}{2}$ cupful of flour, $1\frac{1}{2}$ teaspoonfuls of salt, $\frac{1}{2}$ teaspoonful of nutmeg, 1 tablespoonful of cut parsley. Put the milk on to heat; when it comes to the boiling point set the pan in boiling water. Mix the flour with a little cold water until thick and smooth; to it add the eggs, and beat well for two minutes; then add slowly to the hot milk; add salt, pepper and nutmeg. Cook for three minutes; sprinkle with parsley.

BARLEY BROTH WITHOUT MEAT.

A quarter of a pound of Scotch barley, 2 or 3 onions, sliced, 5 quarts of water. Boil gently for an hour, pour out into another vessel; now melt a lump of dripping in the saucepan and stir into it a quarter of a pound of oatmeal till you bring it to a paste; then add the barley a little at a time, stirring it well together till it boils. Season with a teaspoonful each of pounded celery and ground black pepper, and salt to taste. Let it simmer gently for half an hour and it will be ready. For a small quantity reduce the ingredients proportionately.

FISH SOUP.

Take 2¼ lbs. fish of any kind, wash and skin it, and separate the flesh from the bones. Put into a large saucepan the skin, bones and trimmings, with 2½ quarts water. Bring it to the boil, then add 1 parsnip, 1 carrot, 2 onions, a handful of parsley with the stalks, 1 teaspoon salt, and ½ teaspoon pepper. Boil 1½ hours, till the substance is well extracted, then strain through a colander. Wash the pot and return the liquor to it. Rub 1 tablespoon flour smooth with a little milk, add the rest of the pint of milk and 1 oz. butter, and stir well into the soup. Cut the fish into pieces the size of an oyster, put them in, boil 20 minutes, season to taste, and serve.

PEA-POD SOUP.

Green pea-pods make delicious soup. After shelling peas, wash carefully and prepare the pods and the peas at the same time in order to save fuel. Cover the pods with cold water; add a very small piece of onion; when boiling, set a wire strainer into a saucepan and put the peas into the strainer; boil until tender. Lift out the strainer and pour the peas into a hot dish; add salt, pepper and a little butter; then mash the pods with a wire potato-masher and mash them through a wire strainer. This will make the soup for next day, and one vessel and one fire cooks peas and pods. The sweet pods add to the flavor of the peas, and the water in which the peas have been cooked is not wasted but helps to flavor the cream-of-pea soup for the next day. To each four cupfuls of stock add two table-

spoonfuls of melted butter, two tablespoonfuls of flour, one tablespoonful of sugar, one teaspoonful of salt, pepper to taste and a quarter of a teaspoonful of grated nutmeg. When the stock boils add the butter and flour, rubbed together until smooth, salt and pepper to taste, and boil for five minutes. Half milk and half stock may be used if desired.

PEA SOUP.

Stew a quart of split peas, soaked overnight, in four quarts of good beef broth, for an hour. Pass through a sieve, season to taste, and heat again. A little celery and other suitable vegetables will flavor and improve the soup, and bacon or veal may be cooked with it. Powdered dry mint should be sprinkled in before serving.

FISH

BAKED FISH.

Wash and dry any fish, weighing four or five pounds, dredge with salt and pepper, and place in a buttered pan. Pour over it a quart of chopped tomatoes, a large onion chopped fine, and a large spoonful of chopped parsley. Add a little cayenne pepper and salt. Pour over all one half-cupful of fine oil or melted butter, and then bake slowly until well done.

FISH CAKES.

Take equal weights of fish and potato which has been previously boiled. Break up the fish, free from skin and bone into flakes, and rub the potatoes through a fine sieve. Mix potatoes and fish together and season with salt and cayenne, adding a few drops of anchovy and a squeeze of lemon juice; put all into a basin, and make into a paste with a little milk, melted butter, and a lightly-beaten egg. Make the paste into small round cakes, roll first in a beaten-up egg, and then in breadcrumbs. Fry the cakes until they are golden brown, then serve hot.

FISH MOULD.

Take away all bones and skin from any cold cooked fish and chop into small pieces, mixing in pepper, salt and finely-chopped parsley. Butter some small moulds, and sprinkle with finely-chopped parsley. Put the fish lightly into moulds; make a stiff sauce with two or three eggs well beaten and a very little milk, and pour slowly in to fill up the cups. Cover each with buttered white paper. Stand the cups in a pan of boiling water three-fourths up their sides, and steam until set. Serve hot after carefully turning out, with a suitable sauce.

SCOLLOPED OYSTERS.

This is a favourite dinner dish, and is easy to cook with a little care. Prepare about one pint of cracker or breadcrumbs, butter the dishes (fire-proof china ones are the best), cover the bottom of the dishes with the fine crumbs moistened with oyster liquor; add a layer of oysters, season with pepper and salt, alternate the crumbs and oysters until you have three layers, finish with crumbs, cover the top with small pieces of butter, finish around the edge with bread cut into small oblong pieces dipped in butter; bake half an hour or more if necessary. Serve with sprigs of parsley laid on each dish.

MAYONNAISE OF FISH.

Cut a pound of cold-boiled fish into slices, perhaps an inch in length, and place in a glass or silver dish, with half of the following dressing stirred in with it, the remainder being spread on the top. Dressing:—Mix in a dish the yolks of four hard-boiled eggs, rubbed smooth with salad oil or butter and then add salt, pepper, mustard, two teaspoonfuls of white sugar and, lastly, six tablespoonfuls of vinegar. Beat the mixture well, and, before pouring over the fish, stir in the frothed white of a raw egg. This dish is usually served upon a bed of lettuce leaves.

FISH FRICASSEE.

Take one pound of any white fish, one pint of milk, one blade of mace, rind of half a lemon, six peppercorns, one small onion, one ounce of butter or good clarified fat, one ounce flour, salt. Place the milk, onion, mace, peppercorns and lemon rind in a saucepan, allow to boil slowly, then lay in the fish, cut up in small pieces, and cook very gently for about 15 minutes. Take out the fish, and keep it hot. In another pan leave butter or fat and flour, which fry without browning; then strain on the milk, and boil three or four minutes; just as you remove it from the fire, squeeze in a few drops of lemon juice, now place the fish neatly on a dish, and pour the sauce over it. To decorate add hard-boiled eggs, cut in slices in eight pieces, and put round the dish alternately, with parsley, gherkin and capers. Dust over with pepper before serving.

ENTREES

MACARONI CUTLETS.

One and a half cupful macaroni, 1 cupful white sauce, ¼ pound grated cheese. Cook the macaroni in boiling water and drain it. Make the white sauce and melt the cheese in it; add the macaroni to the sauce, and spread it on a pan to cool. Shape into cutlets; dip them in bread-crumbs, then in beaten egg, and again in bread-crumbs, and fry in a fat until brown. Serve on a platter garnished with parsley.

PILAF WITH CHICKEN.

Pilaf is practically rice cooked in meat stock until the broth is absorbed. This broth or stock can be made from meat, chicken, turkey or game: One small fat chicken, 2 cupfuls of rice, 1 stick of cinnamon, salt and pepper to taste. Boil the chicken in a small amount of water until a rich broth is formed. Strain through a colander; add the rice to the broth, also the cinnamon and, after seasoning it to taste, cook over a strong fire until all the water is evaporated.

Among the different flavors and dressings used to give variety to this national dish, tomato is generally the most acceptable: Five cupfuls of stock, 2 cupfuls of rice, 2 tablespoonfuls of fat, 1 small onion, 4 ripe tomatoes, salt and pepper to taste. Chop the onion very fine and heat it in part of the fat until pink. Place in a deep vessel; add the juice of the tomatoes, also the broth and the rice, which must be well washed. Season to taste and boil until done; pour over the whole the heated fat and place the vessel in a moderately hot oven for from ten to fifteen minutes.

RABBIT WITH POTATO GARNISH.

One rabbit, 3 small onions, 3 garlic cloves, ⅛ teaspoonful thyme, 1 teaspoonful salt, ¼ teaspoonful pepper, 2 cupfuls boiling water. Cut the rabbit in joints, and brown the pieces in a frying-pan with butter, butter substitute or lard. Remove them to a kettle and add the seasonings and boiling water. Let simmer until the rabbit is tender. Add the potatoes, as many as required, and cook until they are done. Serve the rabbit on a platter and garnish it with the potatoes.

MOULDED EGGS WITH CHEESE.

Three eggs, 3 cupfuls milk, ½ pound grated cheese, seasoning. Beat the eggs and milk together and add the grated cheese and seasoning. Pour the mixture into a greased mould and bake it until it is firm. Turn out on a platter, and garnish with chopped parsley.

SMOTHERED SAUSAGE.

To make this toothsome dish, cook the sausages in their own fat until they are deliciously brown and rather crisp, then arrange them in a casserole, pour just a little water over them, and cover thickly with tart apple sliced to correspond to the sausages. Sprinkle the apples with dark brown sugar, then cover the casserole and bake slowly for one hour. Serve, steaming and spicy, in the casserole, placing it on a large plate garnished with parsley.

PUDDINGS

STEAMED BREAD-CRUMB PUDDING.

One cupful of bread-crumbs, ½ cupful of molasses, ¼ cupful of cold water, ¼ cupful of flour, 1 egg, ½ cupful of raisins, 1 teaspoonful of baking soda, 1 teaspoonful of cinnamon, a pinch of cloves, a pinch of salt. Mix all the ingredients thoroughly; put them into a mould or kettle which has been brushed with drippings and steam for three hours. This pudding may be served with either lemon or hard sauce.

PLUM PUDDING.

One cupful each of chopped beef suet, dry breadcrumbs, sugar, flour, seeded raisins, currants; ½ cupful each of finely cut citron, finely cut figs; 1 tablespoonful each of candied lemon peel, candied orange peel; 1 tablespoonful of salt, ¼ teaspoonful each of ground cinnamon, ground cloves, ground ginger, ground nutmeg; 1 cupful of fruit juice. Mix in the order given, and add enough cold water to make a stiff mixture. Brush a mould with butter, fill within one inch of the top, place in boiling water, and boil for eight hours. Remove the lid until the pudding is cold. This may be made two weeks before Christmas. When re-heating boil for one hour. Serve with hard sauce.

DATE PUDDING.

Two cupfuls of milk, 1 cupful of stoned dates, ¼ cupful of sugar, 2 tablespoonfuls of cornflour, ¼ teaspoonful of salt, 1 egg. Heat the milk, and when it comes to a boil add the cornflour, which has been mixed with a little cold milk; then add the sugar, salt, and the egg well beaten; cook for five minutes. While it is cooking wash, stone and cut the dates into thin slices; put them into a glass dish, and pour the pudding over them. Put three or four slices of dates on the top.

STEAMED FRUIT DUMPLING.

Dough: 1 cup sifted flour, ¼ teaspoonful salt, 2 level teaspoonfuls baking powder, 2 level tablespoonful shortening, one-third cup (about) of milk. Filling: 1 cup chopped seeded raisins, 2 tablespoonfuls fine cracker or breadcrumbs, ½ lemon, juice and grated rind, 2 tablespoonfuls sugar.

Sift dry ingredients, rub in shortening, then add milk gradually mixing dough with knife. Turn on to a slightly floured board and roll about one-half inch thick. Cover with raisin filling and roll up as for jelly roll; pinch ends firmly together. Place on a buttered plate and set in a steamer, cover closely and set over boiling water; cook one hour, keeping water constantly boiling. Do not remove cover during cooking or pudding will not be light.

CASTLE PUDDING.

Beat a quarter of a pound of butter and a quarter of a pound of sugar to a cream, add two eggs, with a teaspoonful of flour; beat lightly altogether, taking care they do not curdle, add a quarter of a pound of flour, mixed with half a teaspoonful of baking powder; butter a melon mould, scatter currants over it, pour in the mixture, steam for one hour, and serve with sherry sauce.

CHOCOLATE PUDDING.

Butter a mould; mix a quarter of a pound of plain grated chocolate with a quarter of a pint of milk; boil together to make the chocolate smooth. Beat to a cream a quarter of a pound of castor sugar with three ounces of butter, then stir in the yolks of two eggs and six ounces of fresh white bread-crumbs. Pour on the milk and chocolate, and add a few drops of vanilla. Beat the whites of the two eggs very stiffy, and stir in lightly with the other ingredients. Put the mixture into mould, and steam for one hour. Or bake in a buttered pie-dish for the same time in a slow oven.

FROZEN COCOA PUDDING.

One quart of milk, ¼ cupful of cocoa, 4 tablespoonfuls of cornflour, ¾ cupful of honey, a few grains of salt. Put the milk on into the top of a double boiler; when boiling, add the cocoa and the cornflour, which has been mixed with half a cupful of cold milk. Boil for ten minutes, then add the honey while the pudding is hot. When cold, freeze the same as ice cream. The honey adds an exceptionally good flavor with cocoa or chocolate.

ORANGE TAPIOCA.

Half cupful of orange juice, 1 cupful of sugar, 1½ cupfuls of hot water, 4 tablespoonfuls of powdered tapioca, 1 tablespoonful of lemon juice, a few grains of salt. Put the water into a saucepan; as soon as it boils add the tapioca, stirring slowly all the time; as soon as it begins to thicken add the sugar, salt and lemon juice. When it again thickens, add the orange juice and boil for three minutes. Cool. Serve in ice-cream glasses or a large bowl. Serve with or without cream.

BANANAS WITH LEMON SAUCE.

Six very ripe bananas, 3 tablespoonfuls of lemon juice, 1 teaspoonful of grated lemon rind, 1 egg, $\frac{3}{4}$ cupful of sugar, 1 tablespoonful of flour, 1 cupful of hot water, a pinch of salt. Skin and scrape the fibre from the bananas; slice into a glass bowl, and cover with sauce made as follows: Mix the flour with a little cold water, lemon, almond rind, sugar, pinch of salt and well-beaten egg; add to the hot water; boil until it thickens (about three minutes); pour over the bananas while hot. Let cool before serving. In place of lemon use cherry or any berry juice.

APPLE SNOW WITH CUSTARD.

Two cupfuls of grated raw apple, $\frac{3}{4}$ cupfuls of granulated sugar, $\frac{1}{8}$ teaspoonful of nutmeg, 2 eggs, $\frac{1}{2}$ cupful of milk. To the grated apple add all but one tablespoonful of the sugar; separate the whites of eggs, and beat until dry; then fold into the apples, and add the nutmeg; put into a glass bowl. Beat the yolks of the eggs; add one tablespoonful of sugar, half a cupful of milk and a few grains of salt; put into a small saucepan and bring to the boiling point; remove; flavor to taste; cool and pour around the apple snow.

APPLE FRITTERS.

Six medium-sized cooking apples, 1 cupful of milk, 1 cupful of flour, 2 teaspoonfuls of baking powder, $\frac{1}{2}$ teaspoonful of salt, 2 eggs. Wash, pare and core the apples; cut into rounds a quarter of an inch thick. Dip into the batter and then fry in deep, hot fat or oil. Sprinkle with pulverised sugar. The batter is made as follows: Sift the flour, baking powder and salt into a bowl; add the milk slowly and the well-beaten eggs; mix well, and it is ready for the apples.

CAKES

RICH FRUIT CAKE.

One pound of seedless raisins, one pound of currants, half a pound of finely-sliced citron, half a pound of butter, quarter pint of good brandy, half a pint of molasses, half a pound of brown sugar, one teaspoonful of grated nutmeg, one teaspoonful of ground cinnamon, the same of cloves and mace, six eggs, and half a pound of flour sifted with one teaspoonful of baking soda. Dredge the fruit with flour, stir butter and sugar with a wooden spoon, and add the eggs one at a time, stirring a few minutes between each addition. Next add the molasses, brandy, spice and sifted flour, and lastly stir in the fruit. Butter one large round cake-tin and line it with brown paper, fill in the mixture, and bake in a slow oven from three to four hours. Great care must be taken that the oven is just right.

CARRAWAY CAKE.

Put half a pound of flour in a basin and with the hands rub in four ounces of sweet dripping or butter, a teacupful of brown sugar, and half a teacupful of carraway-seeds, a heaped teaspoonful of baking-powder, and two whole eggs. Mix well together with a little sour milk to a fine dough; well butter a cake-tin or baking sheet, put in the cake mixture, and bake in a hot oven three-quarters of an hour.

RAINBOW CAKE.

Take one pound of sugar and half a pound of butter and beat to a cream. Add six eggs, one at a time, and a small cup of milk. Then add one pound of flour, two tablespoonfuls of cream of tartar, a teaspoonful of carbonate of soda; mix together and beat for a few moments. Then divide the mixture into three equal parts, one flavored with essence of lemon, one flavored with lemon and colored with cochineal, and one flavored with vanilla and colored with four teaspoonfuls of cocoa mixed with water. Bake in sandwich tins for about a quarter of an hour in rather a quick oven. Make an icing as follows:—Two cupfuls of sugar dissolved in a little hot water, boil and stir until it threads from the spoon, beat the whites of two eggs till firm. After boiling the sugar mix it with the whites of eggs, and stir till cool and creamy. Flavor with essence of almond, and then put it between each layer, and on the top afterwards sprinkle ground cocoanut over the whole.

BROWN CAKE (Without Eggs).

Mix together one pound of flour, half a pound of sultanas, quarter of a pound of currants, three ounces of mixed peel, half a pound of castor sugar, one teaspoonful of ground ginger, one teaspoonful of all-spice, one dessert-spoonful of baking soda, six ounces of butter, and one breakfast-cupful of sweet milk. Dissolve the butter in the milk and pour over the dry ingredients, which must be well-mixed. Put into a tin, lined with buttered papers, and bake for about two hours.

SWISS ROLL.

Work four ounces of butter and sifted sugar together for ten minutes, then work in two eggs, one at a time, and six ounces of sifted flour, with a teaspoonful of baking powder well mixed into it, add the flour gradually, and about two tablespoonfuls of milk; work all together for another ten minutes, then pour on to a well-buttered and papered baking sheet and bake in a rather quick oven for fifteen to twenty minutes. Turn on to a wet cloth, cut off the extreme edges of the cake with a sharp knife, spread with jam, and roll up quickly.

COCOANUT DROPS.

Beat half a pound of butter to a cream, and add six ounces of caster sugar to it as you beat, then mix six ounces of desiccated cocoanut to half a pound of flour, and add this to the butter and sugar by degrees; then the whites of the four eggs, beating all the time till they are thoroughly mixed. Then take up little pieces with two forks and drop them on a buttered baking-tin, and bake in a quick oven for about eight minutes.

UK8. Glass Cream Jugs — 1/3 ea.

UK9: Glass Custards — 11½d ea.

UK4. 8½ in. Glass Cake Stand — 2/11 ea.

LEMON JUMBLES.

Mix together one egg, one teaspoonful of sugar, half a teacupful of butter, three teaspoonfuls of milk, a teaspoonful of cream, one of cream of tartar, half a teaspoonful of soda, the juice of two small lemons and the grated peel of one. When the dough is ready roll it out rather thin. Bake in a quick oven for ten minutes.

GINGER-BREAD.

Take three-quarters of a pound of flour, three-quarters of an ounce of ground ginger, half an ounce of carbonate of soda, two ounces of candied peel, quarter of a pound of butter or dripping, quarter of a pound of brown sugar, half a pound of golden syrup, two eggs, and a little milk, if needed. Sieve together the flour, ginger and carbonate of soda. Shred the peel and add it. Put the butter or dripping into a saucepan on the fire to melt; when it is melted, add the sugar and syrup. Allow the sugar to dissolve, but not boil. Make a hole in the flour, and pour in the sugar, etc. When that is partly mixed in and is a little cool, beat up the eggs and add them; then add a little milk if the mixture is too stiff to run quite smoothly into the tin. Cook in a slow oven for about half an hour.

TEA CAKES.

Mix together one pound of flour with two ounces of butter, two large teaspoonfuls of baking powder; mix thoroughly with the flour, then take two eggs and eight tablespoonfuls of milk. Beat the latter together, add to the flour, and mix into a smooth dough; divide into six cakes, and bake in a quick oven for half an hour. Brush the cakes over with the yolk of an egg, which has been beaten up with milk, and a little powdered sugar when they are nearly cooked.

BREAD GRIDDLE CAKES.

One and a half cups stale bread, $1\frac{1}{4}$ cups scalded milk, 2 tablespoons fat, $1\frac{1}{2}$ tablespoons baking powder, 2 eggs, $\frac{1}{4}$ cup flour, $\frac{1}{2}$ teaspoon salt. Add milk and fat to crumbs and soak until crumbs are soft. Add eggs, well beaten; then flour, salt and baking powder, mixed and sifted. Beat. Cook according to general directions.

MERINGUES.

To prevent failures there are several hard-and-fast rules to follow in making these dainties. Both the egg-beater and bowl must be clean and cold. Grease will cause a heavy meringue. All must be cold. Always use the whipping stroke, as stirring releases the air which has been forced in by the egg-beater. Confectioner's sugar, or part confectioner's and granulated, makes the best meringues, but all granulated will make a good meringue. Sift sugar. Meringues cooked too quickly or not enough will fall and liquify. Cool out of drafts.

NUT MERINGUES.

Have ready eight even tablespoons of sifted confectioner's or powdered sugar. Beat the whites of four eggs until stiff and dry, gradually beat in one-half of the sugar. Fold in the remaining sugar, add one-fourth teaspoon of vanilla and one-third cup of finely-broken walnut meats. Drop onto saltines or other crackers and cook in a slow oven until a delicate brown.

KISSES.

Whip the whites of three eggs until stiff and dry, gradually beat in one cup of granulated sugar, remove the egg-beater and fold in one-half cup of powdered sugar and one-half teaspoon of vanilla. Drop by spoonful, well apart, on a wet board covered with writing paper. Bake 30 minutes in a slow oven.

BISCUITS

CRACKNEL BISCUITS.

Take a quart of the best flour, and four yolks of eggs well beaten, in which has been mixed a little nutmeg, a small teacupful of caster sugar, and half a gill of orange or rose-water; pour this into the flour and make a stiff paste. Then roll it out, and work into it by slow degrees a pound of butter, and when thoroughly united roll out to a proper thickness, which is about the third part of an inch, and cut into shapes; throw them into boiling water and let them continue to boil till they swim on the top. They must then be taken out and plunged in cold water to harden, after which they are slowly dried; wash the tops with well-beaten whites of eggs, and bake on tin plates in an oven sufficiently brisk to make them crisp, but by no means too dark a brown.

ALMOND MACAROONS.

Put through a sieve a pound of blanched and dried sweet almonds, make into a rather soft batter with the whites of five or six eggs and a spoonful or two of orange-flower water, beat well, lay the mixture in small lumps on oval wafer-paper, and sprinkle the tops with powdered loaf sugar; bake in rather cool oven.

WALNUT BISCUITS.

Make into a paste a quarter of a pound of butter, half a pound of fine flour, a quarter of a pound of caster sugar, and the yolks of two eggs, and roll out to about a quarter of an inch thick, stamp out with a diamond cutter, brush over with a well-beaten egg, and sprinkle with finely-chopped walnuts, which have been blanched; bake in a moderate oven until a golden brown, and when cold sprinkle with coloured sugar.

SODA BISCUITS.

Take one pound of flour, half a pound of pounded loaf sugar, a quarter of a pound of fresh butter, two eggs, one small teaspoonful of carbonate of soda. Put the flour (well dried) into a basin, rub in the butter, add the sugar, and mix these ingredients well together. Whisk the eggs, stir them into the mixture, and beat it well until everything is well incorporated. Quickly stir in the soda, roll the paste out until it is about half an inch thick, cut it into small round cakes with a tin cutter, and bake them from twelve to eighteen minutes in rather a brisk oven. After the soda is added, great care is necessary in rolling and cutting out the paste, and in putting the biscuits immediately into the oven, or they will be heavy and unfit to eat.

ICE BISCUITS.

Put into a basin two ounces of flour and one ounce of caster sugar, and rub into it till smooth half an ounce of good butter. Mix with this a dessertspoonful of orange-flower water, a saltspoonful of vanilla essence, and one raw yolk of egg, and when perfectly smooth roll it out quite thinly on a floured slab of board; cut the paste in oblong pieces the length of the moulds and broad enough to go round them; arrange these pieces round the tins, which should have been slightly buttered first. Then place them on a sheet of greased foolscap paper on a greased baking-tin, and bake in a moderate oven for fifteen minutes. They should then be a pretty fawn color. Take them up, and when cold take the cases out and set them. Finally, fill with cream as for meringues.

SCOTCH SHORTBREAD.

Put into a warm basin a quarter of a pound of sugar, half a pound of butter, and one pound of flour. Work with the hand until it becomes a firm paste, turn out on to the baking sheet, shape it with the palm of the hand in either rounds or squares, prick with a fork and knit the edges with the finger and thumb; bake in a slow oven.

No. 351.

EGG DISHES

PROGRESSIVE EGGS.

Six hard-boiled eggs, 6 thin slices of toasted bread, 2 cupfuls of milk, 4 tablespoonfuls of butter, 4 tablespoonfuls of flour, 1 tablespoonful of onion juice, 1 teaspoonful of salt, pepper. Make the cream sauce as usual. Chop the whites of the eggs fine, and add to half of the cream sauce; rub five yolks through a strainer, and add to other half of cream sauce; place the toasted bread on hot platter, pile the whites in the centre, and the yolks, in sauce, around the toast. Grate the sixth yolk over all, and garnish with parsley.

RICE AND EGGS.

One cupful of cold boiled rice, 4 eggs, 1 teaspoonful of butter, 4 tablespoonfuls of cold water, 1 tablespoonful of finely-chopped parsley, $\frac{1}{2}$ teaspoonful of salt. Put the butter into a frying pan; when melted pour in the rice, and stir until heated through. Break the eggs into a bowl; add the water, and beat until well mixed; then add the salt, and pour over the hot rice; stir until the eggs are set and firm. Serve on a hot platter, sprinkled with the parsley. A thin grated onion adds to this dish.

DAISY EGGS.

Six eggs, 6 rounds of toasted bread, $\frac{1}{2}$ cupful of milk, $\frac{1}{2}$ teaspoonful of salt, pepper. Butter the toast and put it on a platter or plate which can be put into the oven. Separate the eggs, leaving each yolk separate in a small dish; beat the whites until light; pile the whites on the buttered toasted bread, which has been dipped in cold milk. With the back of a spoon make places in the white of egg and put a yolk in each; place in a hot oven for three minutes or until the eggs are set or baked to your liking. Dust with salt and pepper. Serve at once. This makes a very appetizing dish.

No. 292—Dover Stove.

No. 295—Giffhorn Oven.

No. 294—Littell Stove.

BAKED EGGS IN RICE WITH TOMATO SAUCE.

One cupful of rice, 1 cupful of tomato sauce, 4 eggs, 2 teaspoonfuls of salt. Wash and boil the rice; dust with one teaspoonful of salt, spread on a hot platter, and with the back of a spoon make four places, each to hold one egg. Dust with salt and pepper, place in the oven for five minutes, remove, and cover with the sauce.

DEVILLED EGGS.

Four hard-boiled eggs, 1 teaspoonful of mustard, 1 tablespoonful of butter or olive oil. 1 tablespoonful of vinegar, 1 tablespoonful of cut parsley, a dash of cayenne pepper, 1 teaspoonful of salt. Cut the hard-boiled eggs into halves, lengthwise; remove the yolks, being careful not to break the whites. Powder the yolks with a silver fork; then add the mustard, salt, Cayenne pepper and vinegar mixed together; add the butter, or olive oil, or half a cupful of mayonnaise; mix until smooth, and fill into the whites; rough the tops with a fork. Serve on a bed of lettuce.

BAKED EGGS WITH CHEESE SAUCE.

Four eggs, 1 tablespoonful of grated cheese, 2 tablespoonfuls of butter, 2 tablespoonfuls of flour, 1 cupful of milk, 1 teaspoonful of salt. Brush an earthenware dish with a little butter; break into the dish the four eggs, cover the mixture with cream sauce, and sprinkle it with one tablespoonful of grated cheese. Bake in a hot oven for twelve minutes.

Cream Sauce: Melt the butter; add the flour; mix well, and add the cold milk slowly, stirring until smooth and creamy; add the salt, a little pepper, and boil for two minutes.

OMELETTES

BREAD-CRUMB OMELETTE.

One cupful of dry bread-crumbs, 1 cupful of cold milk, 3 eggs, 2 tablespoonfuls of drippings, 1 teaspoonful of salt. Put the bread-crumbs in a bowl, cover with cold milk and let stand for fifteen minutes; beat the eggs until light; add to the bread, with salt and flavoring to taste; mix well. Put the drippings into a pan; when hot pour in the omelette; do not have the fire too hot; raise the edges to let the soft part go under, and raise the centre; when set, double over. This is good served with jelly between layers and around the omelette.

RICE OMELETTE.

One cupful of cold boiled rice, 1 tablespoonful of drippings, 3 tablespoonfuls of cut onion, 3 eggs, $\frac{1}{2}$ teaspoonful of salt, pepper. Put bacon drippings into a frying pan; fry the onion until tender but do not brown, stirring all the time; add the rice to heat through. Beat the eggs with three tablespoonfuls of cold water until light; add the salt and pepper; pour over the hot rice. Shake the pan constantly; raise the edges so the soft part will run underneath. When set and firm, sprinkle with parsley, and double over. Serve on a hot platter.

OMELETTE FLAVORED WITH DRIED BEEF.

Four eggs, 2 tablespoonfuls of dried beef, 1 teaspoonful of drippings, 4 tablespoonfuls of cold water, a little onion juice, a pinch of salt. Beat the eggs and water until light; add onion juice and salt. Heat the drippings; add eggs; shake pan while frying; when set, add the dried beef, which has been broken into fine pieces and heated. Double the omelette, and serve.

SPANISH OMELETTE.

Four eggs, 2 cupfuls of strained tomatoes, $\frac{1}{2}$ cupful of finely-cut onion, 2 tablespoonfuls of drippings or oil, 2 tablespoonfuls of green pepper, 1 tablespoonful of cut barley, 1 teaspoonful of salt, 1 tablespoonful of flour. Separate the eggs; beat the whites until dry, then the yolks, adding four tablespoonfuls of milk or water; add the well-beaten yolks to the whites, and mix lightly. Have a large pan hot, put in the oil, pour in the egg mixture, and place over a slow fire; cook until set. If the oven is hot put the omelette in; otherwise leave the pan on a slow fire, and cover for a few minutes; it will puff up and cook through. Cover the omelette with sauce, double over, put on platter, and pour the rest of the sauce around.

Sauce: Put one tablespoonful of oil, or drippings, into a pan; add the onion, and boil for a few minutes; then add the tomatoes, salt and green peppers; boil for five minutes; add the flour, which has been mixed with a little cold water. Half a cupful of chopped mushrooms may be added if desired, or a little spice.

OMELETTE WITH BACON CURLS.

Four eggs, $\frac{1}{4}$ pound of thinly-sliced bacon, 2 tablespoonfuls of cold milk, $\frac{1}{2}$ teaspoonful of salt. Fry the bacon quickly in a small frying pan; remove the bacon from the pan, also part of the dripping; separate the eggs, and beat the yolks until light; add the milk and salt; beat the whites of the eggs until they are dry; add to the yolks, and stir lightly; pour into the pan in which the bacon was fried, and cook over a slow fire; with a knife or a spatula raise the edges. Put pan into a hot oven or cover it with a lid or tin pie plate so the eggs will cook; double the omelette, and garnish with the bacon and parsley.

PEPPER OMELETTE.

Beat the yolks of three eggs very light, add a teaspoonful of flour, half a teaspoonful of salt, three tablespoonfuls of cold water, a speck of pepper, and a tablespoonful each of minced red and green sweet pepper. Lastly fold in the stiffly beaten whites and cook as any omelette. Fold, slip onto a hot platter, surround with a little hot tomato sauce, and sprinkle with a bit more of the minced peppers. Serve with hot corn cakes.

RICE OMELETTE.

Rice added to an omelette adds to its nutriment, and makes eggs, when expensive, "go further." Beat the yolks and whites of three eggs separately; to the yolks add one teaspoonful of flour, one-quarter cupful of milk, one-half teaspoonful of salt, two shakes of pepper and, if on hand, one tablespoonful each of minced parsley and any savory, as minced sausage or ham, and one-half cupful of cooked rice. Beat well, fold in the stiffly beaten egg whites, pour into a hot frying pan in which two tablespoonfuls of butter have been melted, let brown lightly on the bottom, then put in a moderate oven a moment to set, fold over, slip onto a hot platter, garnish, and serve. Surround or serve with a hot tomato or Spanish sauce if wished.

SALADS

VEGETABLE SALAD.

One large red beet, boiled; 4 cupfuls of shredded lettuce or cabbage, ½ cupful of mayonnaise dressing, ¼ cupful of French dressing. The red beet is cut into quarter-inch slices; then cut into stars and placed upon the shredded lettuce. On each put a little mayonnaise, and on top of the mayonnaise a tiny star. Serve with French dressing. Tomato aspic can be made, put on a platter to harden, cut with a star cutter and served on lettuce.

LETTUCE SALAD.

The outside of coarse lettuce leaves make delicious salad:—Four cupfuls of outside lettuce leaves, shredded; ¼ cupful of vinegar, 2 tablespoonfuls of finely-cut onion, 2 tablespoonfuls of finely-cut ham fat, 1 tablespoonful of sugar, 1 tablespoonful of salt pepper to taste. Put the ham fat into a pan with the onion, and fry until the onion is tender but not brown; add the vinegar, sugar, salt and a quarter cupful of nut meats or walnuts. Blend the ingredients, moisten well with boiled dressing, and press into small bowls or cups. Place on ice to chill, then turn the salad out in nests of lettuce leaves, and mask the mounds with the dressing. Garnish with rosettes of heart leaves of lettuce.

LOBSTER OR CHICKEN SALAD.

For the first, either fresh boiled or canned lobster may be used; for the second, cold boiled or roast chicken is correct. With either fish or fowl it is well to add at least one-third its quantity of celery cut in small pieces, then bleached in cold water to which a little lemon juice has been added; and hard-cooked eggs, chopped pickles or olives may be added.

EGG AND LETTUCE SALAD.

Lettuce leaves, 4 hard-boiled eggs, French or mayonnaise dressing. Wash and clean the lettuce, breaking it into pieces. Make a bed of lettuce in the salad bowl; shred the whites of eggs very fine and put on top of the lettuce. Mash the yolks through a fruit press, or strainer. Put the yolks one inch around the edge, and heap the remainder in the centre. Cover with dressing. Garnish with slices of pepper.

A LEFT-OVER SALAD.

One cupful of poultry pickings, $\frac{1}{2}$ cupful of finely-cut celery, $\frac{1}{2}$ cupful of mayonnaise, olives, beets or pickles, lettuce. To each cupful of turkey, goose, duck or chicken pickings put through a coarse food chopper add the celery and the mayonnaise; mix well; put into custard cups and set in a cool place. After two or three hours loosen and turn out on shredded lettuce. Garnish with stuffed olives cut into rings, or with beets or pickles.

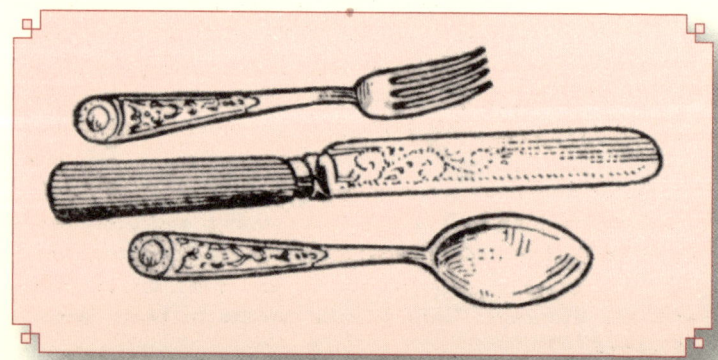

EGG SALAD.

is made almost entirely of hard-cooked eggs chopped coarsely and mixed with mayonnaise or boiled dressing. For variation add beets, celery or potatoes cubed. Cold cooked peas, green pepper, or tiny button radishes halved are also excellent materials with which to vary the plain egg salad.

ROAST BEEF AND POTATO SALAD.

It affords a way of making use of cold roast beef, left-overs or ends of steak which might otherwise go begging. Free the meat from gristle and skin and chop fine. Mix with an equal quantity of chopped boiled potato, add a teaspoonful each of chopped onion and parsley and two or three Spanish olives chopped. Moisten well with any dressing that may please you. Half a teaspoonful of mustard or horse-radish mixed with the French dressing provides a tasty dressing for this salad.

BANANA SALAD.

Six ripe bananas, 2 cupfuls of shredded lettuce, $\frac{1}{2}$ cupful of French dressing. Skin and scrape the fibre from the bananas; cut them into thin slices, place them on the shredded lettuce, and cover them with French dressing at once. The reason for shredding lettuce is that none will be wasted; the good outside leaves are mixed with the tender centres and each portion will be the same, and it is much easier to manipulate when at the table.

French dressing is made by mixing thoroughly one part vinegar or lemon juice with three parts olive oil and seasoning it with onion juice, salt and pepper.

SALAD CAMBRISSON.

Beef left-overs, two eggs, hard-boiled; one small head of lettuce, 2 tomatoes, 4 anchovies. Cut the beef in small pieces, add the eggs and tomatoes cut in slices, and anchovies in small pieces. Serve on lettuce with dressing.

AA 7X.— Glucose Barley Sugar. PRICE, per jar .. 1/-

AA 3X.—Minties.
PRICE, per lb. 1/9

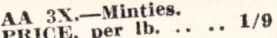

AA 5 X.— Cadbury's Selected Chocolates.
PRICES, per tin.
½lb. 2/-
1lb. 4/-

AA 6X.—Old Gold Chocolates.
½lb. box 2/-
1lb. box 4/-

CONFECTIONERY

FONDANTS.

Fondant is considered the foundation for all French bonbons and for chocolate creams. It will keep several weeks if properly packed in an air-tight jar lined with waxed paper.

French-Cream Fondant: Two cupfuls of sugar; one cupful of water. Stir the sugar and water together until mixed; do not stir at all after it has come to the boiling point, and not more than three times before; stir only enough to prevent sticking at the bottom; boil until a soft ball forms when dropped into cold water; remove from the fire, and place pan in a pan of cold water. Allow the mixture to stand until cool; add half a teaspoonful of vanilla; then beat until it forms a white mass which leaves the edge of the pan; knead well until perfectly smooth and absolutely no hard grains remain.

CHOCOLATE CREAMS.

The basis of a chocolate cream is fondant. Prepare the French-Cream Fondant as given here. This fondant may be made in large quantities and kept indefinitely by placing it in waxed air-tight jars. There are various methods of coating chocolate creams. A very successful home method, simple and delicious, is the following:

Place four or more squares of unsweetened chocolate in a small china bowl. Place the bowl in a pan of boiling water, and allow the chocolate to melt. The fondant is formed into desired shapes and allowed to stand for several hours. With a silver fork drop the fondant into the melted chocolate. When nicely covered on all sides remove to a piece of waxed paper, and, by allowing chocolate to drip from end of fork directly across the centre of the top, you form the line which is significant of "hand-dipped." One coating of chocolate is usually sufficient.

PENUCHE.

Put two tablespoonfuls of butter in a granite-ware or aluminium saucepan. When melted, add two cupfuls of brown sugar and one-third cupful of cream or rich milk.

Bring to the boiling-point and boil until the soft-ball state, about twelve minutes. Take from the fire, add three-fourths of a cupful of chopped peanuts or English walnuts and beat until creamy. Pour into a buttered tin. Cool slightly and work in squares.

PEANUT CREAMS.

A little jar of popular peanut butter is the first requisite. This is slightly salted, then shaped in any form desired. Have ready some melted chocolate in one shallow dish, some fondant in another, some chopped nutmeats in a third, some stoned dates and steamed prunes with the stones removed in a fourth, with chopped figs and raisins in the fifth. Roll the peanut butter forms in some of these, which will serve as delectable covers, and insert smaller pieces of the butter in the dates and prunes.

DATE AND COCOANUT SWEETS.

Two cupfuls of dates, after stoning; 1 cupful of canned grated cocoanut, $\frac{1}{2}$ teaspoonful of salt, 1 tablespoonful of lemon juice, 4 tablespoonfuls of sugar.

Wash, dry and put the dates through a food chopper. Add the salt, together with three-quarters of a cupful of cocoanut and the lemon juice. Mix the ingredients well; then form the mixture into round balls and roll them in cocoanut and sugar.

AFTER-DINNER CREAM NUTS.

Two cupfuls of granulated sugar, two-thirds cupful of water, $\frac{1}{2}$ teaspoonful of peppermint, a pinch of baking soda.

Boil the sugar and water together until they form a soft ball when dropped into cold water. Remove from the fire; add the baking soda, and heat until the mixture begins to get hard. Then add the mint. When thick, drop with a teaspoon on waxed paper or on a buttered platter. Set away in a cool, dry place to dry.

PEANUT MOLASSES CANDY.

Place in a good-sized kettle one quart of good molasses, one cup of sugar and one-quarter cup of butter. Boil rapidly, stirring constantly, until it will snap sharply in ice water, then add a level teaspoon of baking soda and stir a moment. Have ready one quart of peanuts, which have been shelled, skinned and broken apart into halves. Add them to the candy and stir rapidly and just enough to mix well, and pour at once into flat, square, greased pans. When partly cold mark into blocks and cut through. If wrapped neatly in waxed paper and kept in a dry place this will keep nicely for weeks.

TAFFY APPLES.

Cook syrup made from one cup white sugar, one cup brown sugar, one-half cup vinegar and one-half cup water until it will crack when dropped in cold water.

Select firm, red apples, wipe, and insert wood skewer. Dip entire apple in syrup until well coated. Skewer is left in to hold apple by when eating. Apples are merely coated, not cooked. These are much beloved by youngsters and are an excellent substitute for candy.

BUTTER SCOTCH.

Boil three cups of brown sugar and three-fourths cup of water until the syrup will form a thread when dropped from the spoon; add two tablespoonfuls of butter and one-eighth teaspoonful of soda, boil a minute longer, then add a teaspoonful of vanilla or any preferred flavoring, pour into hot, buttered pans, crease when slightly cool, and let stand until hard.

CORDIALS

GINGER WINE.

To make ten gallons of ginger wine, take eight gallons and five pints of water, twenty-four pounds of loaf sugar, thirteen and a half ounces of ginger, four pounds of raisins, eight Seville oranges, six tablespoonfuls of yeast. Bruise the ginger, and boil the ingredients half an hour; let it stand till nearly cold, then put it into the cask with the juice of the oranges, raisins and yeast chopped small. Let it stand six or seven days, put in half an ounce of isinglass and a quartern of the best brandy. Bung up the cask and let it stand three months, then bottle off.

HOP BEER.

Boil five ounces of hops slowly in nine gallons of water for about three-quarters of an hour. Strain over three pounds of brown sugar in a large pan, add a little bruised ginger, and when luke-warm add about three or four tablespoonfuls of yeast, and let it ferment. If this is to be kept, add a little brandy, for it is not easy to keep any fluid containing sugar without it. After twenty-four hours, strain off and bottle, tie down the corks tightly, or draw from a stone or wooden cask as required for use.

BLACKBERRY CORDIAL.

Wash and pick over the berries; mash with a wooden spoon in a preserving kettle; let them come to a boil; strain; to every pint of juice add ½ pint water, 1 pound loaf sugar, 1 ounce each of cloves, mace, and cinnamon. 1 grated nutmeg, 1 ounce pounded green ginger; boil ½ hour; strain, and when cool add to each pint 1 gill of brandy. Keep in a cool dry place.

RASPBERRY SYRUP.

Steep the raspberries in vinegar, allowing one pound of raspberries to three pints of vinegar. This should be done in a glazed earthenware vessel, and should stand for eight or ten days in a cold cellar. Strain through muslin, and add one and a half pounds of sugar. Boil for ten minutes and finish off as before. Raspberries can be prepared for the same thing without vinegar, thus:—Crush the fruit in a wooden bowl, stand it in the cellar lightly covered up, and leave it there to ferment. The juice should be a bright clear pink. Strain it as above, and to every pint of juice allow a good pound of sugar. The latter should be put over the fire in the liquid, and as soon as the former is quite melted the syrup is ready.

LEMONADE.

Take two lemons, pare thinly off a little of the peel, or rub lumps of sugar upon it; squeeze out the juice of the fruit, and mix it with two ounces of white sugar, including what has been rubbed upon the lemons; add boiling-hot water, and when cool enough strain the liquor. Dilute the preparation with water to the strength desired. Should lemons not be in season syrup of lemons may be used, or crystallised citric acid and sugar, adding a few drops of essence of lemon.

STONE JAR GINGER BEER.

Pour two gallons of boiling water over two and a half pounds of loaf sugar, two ounces of crushed ginger, the peel and juice of two lemons, with half an ounce of cream of tartar; cover the pan, and leave till nearly cool. Add two tablespoonfuls of yeast, and leave it to ferment for two days; then strain it, and bottle in small bottles with the corks securely wired down.

Crystal Goblet Sets
Reflecting Exquisite Taste

CA 301X.—Full Lead Crystal Goblet Sets, assorted shapes and cuttings.
PRICES, set 45/-, 48/6, 59/6
With Low Footed Goblets.
PRICE, set **42/6**
Also **Water Sets.**
PRICES, ... 38/6, 45/-, 49/6, to 65/-

The New Lager Sets, plain cut, with tall jug and tumblers to match.
PRICES, set 66/-, 78/6, 92/6
Whisky Sets. PRICES 39/6, 42/6, 47/6
Light Cut Water Sets, with Georgian shape tumblers.
PRICE, set **15/-**

JAMS

MELON AND LEMON JAM.

To twenty pounds of melon allow twelve pounds of sugar, six lemons and one pint of lime-water. Peel the lemons, using only the outer part, free from seeds. Slice, and cut the slices into cubes or blocks half-inch every way. Put into an earthenware pan, sprinkle the fruit with three pounds of sugar, pour the lime-water over, and let it remain all night. Next morning strain off the liquid and boil for half an hour to reduce the quantity, then put the melon in and boil till tender, then add the grated rind and juice of the six lemons with the remainder of the sugar. All must now be boiled well together, stirred constantly, and the scum taken off as it rises. Try a little of the mixture on a plate. When it jellies, the jam is cooked. Some makers add a little citric acid and a small quantity of essence of lemon.

PLUM JAM.

Do not forget that when the plums are very hard and sour, a larger proportion of sugar will be required. Cut the plums in halves and take out the stones; or stab them with a silver knife and remove the stones as they rise in the pan. Spread the plums out on large dishes, strew over them three pounds of sugar to every four pound of fruit, and leave for twenty-four hours. Put them into a preserving-pan, and bring slowly to a boil, stirring them with a wooden spoon to keep them from burning. Remove the scum as it rises, then boil quickly for half an hour. If liked, a few of the stones can be cracked, and the kernels peeled and added to the jam two or three minutes before the jam is taken from the fire. When the jam sets and the plums are soft, the jam is cooked. Place a round of thin paper dipped in brandy on the top of the jam. Cut some rounds of paper large enough to overlap the top of the jar about an inch. Brush the inside with beaten white of egg, or a little gum, and tie it on whilst wet. This will keep out the air.

STRAWBERRY JAM.

Allow a pound of sugar to a pound of strawberries, weighed after they have been stalked. Select fruit that is ripe, but sound. Stalk the strawberries, weigh them, and put them into a preserving-pan, with their weight in loaf sugar; bring to the boil, and then put the pan where it will cook gently, without boiling too rapidly. Remove all scum as it rises, and stir the fruit now and then, or it will stick to the bottom of the pan and burn. Be careful not to break up the strawberries if you can possibly keep them whole. After it comes to the boil it will take about forty-five minutes to cook. Try it by pouring a little on a plate, when, if it sets it is cooked. Pour the jam into clean dry jars, and, when cold, cover tightly.

ORANGE MARMALADE.

One pound peeled oranges, ¼ lb. peel removed from oranges, 1 quart water, 14 oz. sugar.

Wash fruit, remove one-fourth of the peel (free from blemish) and cut into slices, as thin as possible. Cover with water and boil ten minutes. Drain. Repeat this process twice, cooking in the last water until tender.

With a sharp knife, remove and discard the yellow part from the skin which remains on the oranges. Leave the white part on, for it contains the pectin. Weigh the fruit, cut it into small pieces. For each pound of fruit, weigh 14 ounces of sugar. Put the fruit into a preserving kettle and add one quart cold water. Bring to a boil and cook until the fruit thoroughly disintegrates—about 20

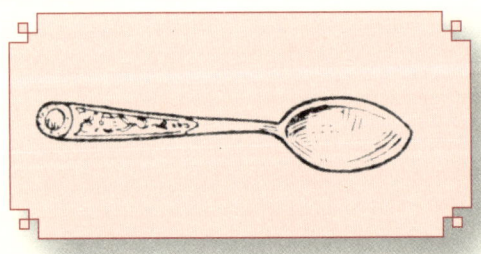

minutes. Pour into a jelly bag and press free from juice. Discard the pulp. Bring the juice to a boil, add the weighed sugar and cooked peel and cook until it flakes or sheets from the spoon.

If very ripe oranges are used, add the juice of one lemon to each pound of fruit.

APPLE MARMALADE.

Cut up apples without paring or coring and just barely cover with cold water in a preserving kettle. Boil to a mush, stirring and mashing often, and drain in jelly bags. To each quart of juice allow three-quarters measure of sugar, which should be heated. Add to three quarts of the juice one-quarter cupful of vinegar, two oranges sliced in thin slivers, and if liked a rose geranium leaf and a small bag of mixed spices. Boil hard eight minutes, then add the hot sugar, and boil five minutes more. When filling the glasses, part of the juice may be strained through cheesecloth if wished, making a clear, highly flavored jelly; the remainder will form a rather thicker marmalade which will jelly, but be of an entirely different consistency from the ordinary marmalade.

CARROT MARMALADE.

Three cups carrots, $\frac{1}{2}$ teaspoonful salt, 4 cups sugar, 2 oranges, 3 lemons, 1 cup water.

Wash carrots, scrape, grind or chop, then cook until tender. Wash and peel oranges, putting one peeling through the food chopper; the other, cut into fine strips. Boil these until tender, in water to cover. Cut the orange pulp in small pieces. Squeeze the juice from the lemons. To the hot carrots add sugar, allowing it to melt. Then add water, lemon juice, orange pulp and cooked peeling. Cook until syrup is thick and fruit clear.

Three slices of canned pineapple may be substituted for the orange pulp.

Some people like to add spices in the proportion of one tablespoon of cinnamon, ginger and allspice, to 6 pounds of the vegetable.

PRESERVED PEARS.

Take some sound, ripe fruit. Peel and halve the pears, core and cut out each blossom, taking care to keep each steam, and drop into cold water until all are ready. To each pound of fruit weighed allow three-quarters of a pound of sugar, and put the peels into an enamelled saucepan with a pint of water and boil for half an hour. Strain, and to this juice add enough water to allow one pint for every two pounds of sugar, and to each pint add half an ounce of green ginger and a little lemon juice. Boil this syrup and remove all scum as it rises, take out the ginger, wash it in warm water, and return it to the syrup. Drain the pears and simmer in the syrup till soft enough to be pierced with a straw. When cooked take out each piece carefully and place in jars, cover with boiling hot syrup. Cover at once.

APPLE JELLY.

Pare, core, and slice the apples. Boil the slices in a little water till they are pulpy; strain them through a hair-sieve; that which runs through is to be used. Take one pound of lump sugar for each pint of juice, and boil for twenty minutes. The juice of a lemon with a bit of sugar may be boiled along with it. Pour into jars, and cover tightly when cold.

PICKLES

PICKLED RED CABBAGE.

Choose a firm, hard cabbage; remove the outer leaves, and cut it as finely as possible in cross slices. Put it in a large shallow dish, with a layer of salt spread over it, and leave it for twenty-four hours; then squeeze the juice thoroughly from it, and place in pickle jars, putting between every handful a little black pepper and bruised ginger. Fill the jars with cold vinegar, or, better still, vinegar that has been boiled and allowed to become cold, and cork securely. It is ready for use at once.

CHOW-CHOW.

Four quarts of green tomatoes, 1 medium-size cabbage, 6 large onions, 12 green cucumbers, 2 stalks of celery.

Chop the vegetables together and lay in a preserving kettle with salt sprinkled lightly between the layers. Let stand overnight. Drain off the brine and cover with vinegar and water—half and half—and let stand twelve more hours. Then drain again and cover with three quarts of scalding vinegar in which has been boiled:

A quarter-pound of mustard seed, 1 tablespoonful each of black pepper, cinnamon and tumeric, 1 cupful of granulated horse-radish, 2 pounds of granulated sugar.

Let stand overnight and in the morning add: One cupful of salad oil, $\frac{1}{4}$ pound of ground mustard.

Mix well and put in jars.

CHUTNEY SAUCE.

Twelve green sour apples, 2 green peppers, 6 green tomatoes, 4 small onions, 1 cupful of seeded raisins, 1 quart of vinegar, 2 tablespoonfuls of mustard seed, 2 tablespoonfuls of salt, 1 tablespoonful of powdered sugar, 2 cupfuls of brown sugar.

Chop tomatoes, peppers, onions and raisins; boil the vinegar, sugar and spices, add to the chopped ingredients and simmer for one hour; add the apples, pared, cored and chopped; cook slowly until the apples are soft. Keep in small bottles, well corked.

If one likes the flavor of mint, a tablespoonful of mint leaves, finely chopped, added with the apples, makes this chutney a very good accompaniment to roast lamb.

PICKLED ONIONS.

Use small white onions. Remove the ends and outer skin and wash thoroughly; cover with brine, allowing three-quarters of a cupful of salt to one quart of boiling water; let stand twenty-four hours. Pour off the brine and cover again with new brine half as strong; boil with the onions two or three minutes and then drain. Pack the onions in jars with small strips of red pepper, a few cloves and bits of whole mace; fill the jars with scalding vinegar in which has been boiled half a cupful of sugar to every two quarts of vinegar; seal while hot.

TOMATO SAUCE.

Tomato sauce of a particularly savory kind may be prepared by trying out one tablespoonful of finely minced fat salt pork, in which saute one-half each of a small carrot, turnip and green sweet pepper, one small onion and a bit of smarty pepper—all finely minced—for about five minutes. Add three quarts of cut-up tomatoes—unskinned—two cloves and a sprig each of parsley and celery; cover and cook until soft—about three-quarters of an hour. Remove parsley and celery, and rub all possible through a sieve. Return to stove, season highly with about one and one-half teaspoonfuls of salt, one teaspoonful of sugar, and pepper and cayenne depending upon the amount of smarty pepper used above; let boil up. This sauce may be canned, boiling hot. When used it may be enriched by thickening very slightly with one teaspoonful of butter melted with half a teaspoonful of flour to a cupful of the sauce. During the tomato season I consider this sauce a real staple.

GREEN-TOMATO PICKLE.

One peck of sliced tomatoes, 6 large sliced onions, 1 cupful of salt.

Mix together and let stand overnight. In the morning drain and add two quarts of vinegar and boil fifteen minutes; drain again and throw away the vinegar; add:

Two pounds of granulated sugar, 2 quarts of vinegar, 2 tablespoonfuls each of ground cloves, ground allspice, and ground cinnamon, $1\frac{1}{2}$ tablespoonfuls of ginger, $2\frac{1}{4}$ tablespoonfuls of mustard seed, 1 scant teaspoonful of cayenne pepper.

Boil for fifteen minutes and store in a stone crock carefully covered, or seal in glass jars if preferred.

KETCHUP.

Half a bushel of ripe tomatoes; be sure that they are dark red and fair. Cut up and boil, unskinned, in a large preserving kettle, adding six onions and three red sweet peppers—seeds removed—all of which have been run through meat chopper. Also add a loosely tied bag of mixed spices—whole cloves, stick cinnamon, allspice buds, one-quarter pound in all—and boil rapidly until tomatoes are very soft, mashing frequently. Strain through a sieve. Return to stove and add three-quarters of a cupful of salt, three cupfuls of brown sugar, one saltspoonful of cayenne, half a nutmeg, grated; one tablespoonful of mustard—mix these ingredients with the sugar to prevent lumping—add three cupfuls of very strong vinegar, one quart if milder. Boil rapidly until reduced about one-third, stirring often. Can, boiling, in sterilized pint jars, or cool and bottle.

Things To Think About

Look up.
Fear is failure.
Go on cheerfully.
Kind creates kind.
Not to believe is half to fail.
Any faith makes for happiness.
To-day is the son of Yesterday.
He who loves most is the master.
Dreams make a pattern for living.
A step at a time will end any climb.
To be afraid is never justified to God.
Life is only as complex as we make it.
"I will" is no harder to say than "I can't."
There is a hint of eternity in every moment.
A man is only as strong as his essential spirit.
Health is sacred and wholeness is holiness:
Beware of selfishness; it can make you cruel.
Beauty is an open letter of recommendation.
When the heart is empty the head grows busier.
A gilded figurehead never made a ship sail faster.
You cannot advance while you are looking back.

Things Which Count in Dress

COLOR — The Part it Plays In Nature and In Our Lives

Look out at Nature. Note her lavish use of colour. Its glory is a constant appeal to our sense of the beautiful.

Can you not feel the quite cheerfulness in the blue of a clear sky, the splashes of golden sunlight and the purpling shadows? You can also feel grateful for the living green of growing plants—rested in the soft grey of light clouds of the distant horizon or disturbed and depressed by the leaden tones of heavy smoke or the murk of a coming storm. The beauty of the colors on a bird's or a butterfly's wing, in the petals of a flower, in the sky at sunset are all inspiring and cheering, and help to drive home the thought that "God's in His Heaven, all's well with the World."

Every season has its message told in color—

The Spring opens with the pale yellow of primrose, soft pink and baby blue of the early blossoms and the tender green of the young leaf buds. As the season grows in warmth there comes richer yellows, pinks, reds and blues. The trees and grass take on a stronger green.

With Midsummer, pink is less frequent, giving place to more yellow. Deeper mauves and purples are evident. Ripe fruit joins in the chorus of color as the season turns.

Then comes the symphony of russet, orange and purple.

After the fall of the Autumn leaves the brilliancy in Nature's color grows less, but keeps its note in the redness of berries, and the gold of winter sunsets.

The bare trees are brown, the evergreens are dark against the mantle of snow which falls in the colder districts. The quiet blues and purples of violets with the white of jonquils and snowdrops tell of a time of rest before the new birth of the coming Spring.

All this has a meaning and meets with its response in the human heart.

The important part color plays in the lives of the people is shown in all classes of the community. The rich and cultured garb, their women richly using aesthetic color schemes. They plant gardens and pay high wages to have them tended and keep blooming the flowers that only care can maintain. They spend large sums of money on pictures, china, and costly decorations to please their sense of color. The untutored fill their houses and adorn their persons with color that they find pleasing but may not be equally so to those of greater knowledge. The inhabitants of even the poorest and most squalid districts in our crowded cities, or the folks with the hardest struggling lives out in the back blocks, show their love of color in various ways—by a plant blooming brightly in spite of dingy surroundings, by prints of pictures cut from various periodicals or by gaily colored, if poor materials, in their clothing, curtains and furnishings.

Note the effect of color on children. Babies, especially girls, will very early reach out to clutch the colored ribbons on their mother's nightdresses and eagerly grasp flowers or other bright hued articles. They will go readily to a woman or child in a pretty, bright colored frock, but will cry bitterly when approached or spoken to by a woman in sombre black, particularly when an unrelieved toilette is surmounted by a heavy black hat or bonnet.

Children should be dressed in cheerful colors. To get the best mental effect from color, they should themselves be satisfied with the hues they are asked to wear. Their natural instincts, unspoiled by fashion or prejudice, will assist them in approving the colors most necessary to their temperament and development. If your little girl wants to wear a ribbon of some particular color, humour her by letting her do so, even if it is only when playing about in the garden at home. Do not punish her for being unreasonable in wishing to express her personality in this way.

Dress children in colors most likely to help self expression. Do not overpower a diffident little girl by covering her with brown or slate grey. Even navy blue, on such a child should be a bright one and have the relief of at least a white collar. Better dress her in cheerful yellows, blues, greens or rose pink and watch her expand and blossom as she should. Do not dress a vociferous boy in a red velvet suit and expect him to behave quietly, nor an effeminate boy in pale blue and expect him to be properly manly.

Surround children with harmonious and beautiful colors, in fact with beauty on all sides, as far as possible. Tasteful color, as well as beauty of surrounding and thought, is ennobling as well as inspiring, just as ugliness and squalor are dispiriting.

THE MENTAL EFFECT OF COLOR.

Orange is the warmest color and blue the coldest. Reds and yellows and browns are warm in proportion as they approach orange. Purples, greens and browns are cool in proportion as they approach blue. White, black and grey are warm or cool in the same way. A neutral black, white or grey look warm against cool colors or cool against warm colors by contrast. This is an important point to remember in making up color schemes for dress designing.

The warm colors have an enlivening and exciting effect on the mentality of the wearer and the beholder. Scarlet is recognised as the color of passion and excitement. Greens and warm greys, on the other hand, have a refreshing and soothing effect and heavy purples, leaden greys and heavy dull blues are depressing when unrelieved.

LADIES' BAGS

6.—Handsome Black Seal Bag, lined with the finest art. silk moire. The flap is edged with white, and has a high-class enamel ornament attached. This bag is fitted with a gusseted front pocket, a 5 x 2½ mirror, and a sensible flat purse with gussets. The frame is covered and the handle expands. This bag is emphatically superior and exclusive, combining the Bunch and Wallet Bag in one.

71.—A medium size and very fashionable Bag. Generally made in finest crocodile calf, which is so effective that it cannot be detected from the real crocodile. It is mounted on a triple frame, assorted catches, swing inner frame with divided pocket. Fitted with purse and mirror, and has a gusset all round. Lined poplin moire. This bag is excellent quality, and is very smart. Size, 10 x 7.

38.—Top Opening Bag. A very popular shape on triple frame, supplied with various catches. Lined with good poplin moire. Fitted with divided centre frame, purse, and mirror. Made in yearling calf and morocco. Size, 10 x 7.

37.—A Pleated Bunch Bag with top opening. Fitted with triple frame, double opening with centre, which is divided. Lined with poplin moire, and has mirror and purse inside. Made in yearling calf, with centre panel of crocodile calf; also in all the popular colours in morocco. It has a gusset all round, and is a smart, useful bag with a great capacity.

Not only are Simpson's Bags extremely fashionable but the excellence of their make causes continual favourable comment

41.—This Bag is made up with a triple frame, and is a very popular line. A gusset right round the bag makes it very roomy. Centre pleats are in contrasting colour, which makes a very smart finish. Fitted with a divided two-colour centre pocket; also mirror and purse. Lined with poplin moire.

CHOOSING YOUR OWN COLOR SCHEMES.

The savage and semi-civilized woman decks herself in gaudy feathers and beads and dyes her ornaments and her more or less scanty clothing in the crudest of colors. Her civilized sister devises more subtle color harmonies. The greater her advancement the more restrained and surer her taste. The well dressed woman of to-day makes her color selection attractive because she makes it accessory to her personality.

The choice of the colors a woman should wear is a matter for thought and judgment rather than for fancy and preference.

It is, of course, one of the great secrets of dressing becomingly, to wear colors suitable to yourself—your natural coloring at the time of wearing, your age, appearance, surroundings, occupation, time of year and good usage.

Let us first take your natural coloring at the time of wearing. Many women continue to wear in middle life, the colors which suited them in their youth, without taking into account the fact that their coloring has been gradually altering and now calls for a different setting. Remember that the colors you wear must accentuate your good points and minimise your defects.

Take account of your complexion, your hair and your eyes, their importance is in this order: A good clear skin, neither too red nor too pale, as long as it has no touch of sallowness, is ideal, and makes the color choice easy. Practically all colors go with such complexions. Aim at the freshness that goes with good health and an exquisite skin—it is worth more than jewels, costly furs or the richest materials. With it you may wear the fashionable colors and with the right silhouette cannot fail to attain smartness. The exceptions to this are when eyes are faded, lustreless or of very pale color, or when the hair is red or drab. But most of us are not endowed with a perfect complexion and it is fortunate that there are usually so many shades and variations in the fashionable colors that there seems to be always something among them in which we may look presentable.

As a general rule, provided eyes and hair permit, the following general rules are safe to observe—they are chiefly what not to wear. The florid should avoid tones of red, rose, pink, lavender and purple. Orange, yellow, henna, tomato, tangerine, tango and tan are to be sparingly used, and then chosen with great care. The best colors for this complexion are black, navy, dark green, grey, blue, grey green, grey, smoke, mole, cool brown, cream, putty, beige, dove, oyster and true white.

The too pale should avoid strong sapphire blue, emerald green, mustard, orange, cherry, tan, canary and dead white, but may wear black relieved with color, navy blue, brown all but the yellow tones, reseda green, wine, flesh pink, mole, grey blue, cream and ivory when relieved with color or with black.

Women with sallow skins are more difficult to suit. They should avoid black, unless relieved with white or cream near the face, purple, navy with a purple tinge, strong greens, red or yellow browns, slate, scarlet, sapphire, rose, cherry, orange, canary, tan and dead white. The best colors are navy blue of good rich color, warm medium grey, mole, grey blue, grey green, grey amethyst, grey fawn, dark green, cream and old rose, with a dull tone.

Blonds may wear pale pastel shades, and brunettes the bright tones in the colors that suit them.

Black hair does not look its best with black or navy blue, but is enhanced by all other colors.

Brown hair is greatly helped by a touch of brown in the dress or hat, bright blues or greens also show up its color, but black unrelieved is not helpful. All bright and pale colors will bring out the color in real brown hair.

Where hair is between colors, strong blues, greens, browns and yellows have a tendency to reduce its color, but black, navy, dark green and light colors are good.

Red hair is lovely with black, blues, greens, greys, cool dull browns, primrose, champagne, dove, oyster, white, cream, mole or fawn, but never red brown or mustard shades, red, mauve, red purple or wine. Tomato, orange or gold may be used in just a touch to repeat the hair color, but with great judgment.

Golden hair looks well in most colors, but is not enhanced by cherry, strong rose, crimson, wine, mustard or tan. It is lovely with black, navy and green, and ash blonde is best with black, dark blues, greens, medium browns, light greys, bright red, yellow, white, old rose, cherry and apricot.

When the hair is drab or indeterminate in color or turning grey, it is advisable to refrain from wearing brilliant colors.

The woman with prematurely white or really grey hair, provided that her age appearance permits, allowing for the color of her complexion, may wear any color. Black is lovely with quite white hair, so are all pale colors.

Bright, healthy eyes of any definite color are an asset and are not detracted from by any color. Nevertheless their attractiveness is distinctly enhanced by repeating their color in some portion of the dress.

The owner of dull, lustreless or pale colored eyes must avoid bright colors which have a tendency to make them still less telling.

Age appearance is an important consideration in choosing the colors in dress. It is not necessarily the number of years that counts with a woman. Character, health, temperament, intellecct and cheerfulness may all make a woman of forty look younger than another of thirty or one of sixty or seventy younger than another at fifty. Some of them have a youthful spirit persisting throughout their life. A woman no longer young looking will discard the youthful colors of her girlhood, but she may still wear cheerful colors with touches of really bright ones.

The time has passed when every woman from middle life, onwards, condemned herself to black. Navy blue has become the standard color, and is far more generally becoming, and makes women look younger instead of older. But then, navy is favoured by women of all ages.

Brown and dark green are also good and becoming dark colors for standard wear.

Navy blue in various forms, especially when avoiding the purple tones, is extremely useful and a few garments to harmonise will give the effects of quite an extensive wardrobe.

With a tailored suit in this color, there can be a plain and a dressy hat which will harmonise, a jumper, a fancy overblouse, a front or two and some crepe-de-chene, silk or muslin blouses of white, flesh or beige color. These, with a topcoat will make a very complete set of outer wear.

The purpose for which a garment is intended helps to decide its color, also the surroundings where it will be worn. One does not buy pale or bright colors for tailored suits nor dull browns for evening wear. Sports and holiday clothes should be of festive colors.

Temperament, too, is to be considered. A shy, retiring woman is not well clothed in brilliant colors, and a bolyant and vivacious one does not look right in all neutral tones.

Stout women no longer are forever told to wear black. They may wear any unobtrusive color as long as the line is right.

Where you must wear a color which is not most becoming, try, as far as possible, to have it cut low or to wear it with white or cream near the face, or, if not, have a string of white beads round the neck to soften the colour.

The black, which is unbecoming to many women, is the dull black of many woollen materials. Rich, lustrous black, particularly in silks and velvets, reflect the surrounding lights and colors and is often most becoming.

A Chart of Correct Colors and Color Combinations for Different Types of Women

	Real Blond	†Robust Blond	*Real Brunette	Real Brunette	White or grey	White or grey
The Type	Real Blond, good, clear healthy complexion, eyes any color if clear and brilliant.	†Blond lacking brilliancy in hair or in eyes of any color or both and complexion slightly sallow.	*Real Brunette, good clear, healthy complexion, eyes any color if clear and brilliant.	Real Brunette, skin slightly sallow, eyes any color.	White or grey hair premature or natural, good healthy complexion, eyes any color if clear and brilliant.	White or grey hair with sallow complexion, eyes lacking color and brilliancy.
Blue	All tones from dark to light including greyed blues, and blues showing their combination with green like peacock and turquoise.	All tones except those tones showing green or purple tint.	Dark tones only.	All tones.	All tones except light tones and those with green tint.	All tones except "baby" blue for the mature.	Dark tones, only avoid purple or green tint.

Brown	All tones except light tans.	Only dark tones.	All tones except tans and those tones having a yellow tint, green or bronze tint are good.	All tones.	Only dark tones of rich warm quality and no tint of yellow or green.	All tones.	No.
Green	All tones.	No.	All tones.	All tones.	No.	Dark tones.	No.
Purple	All tones from Royal to lavender and orchid.	Yes, except Royal and pale lavender.	All tones.	All tones.	Plum and grape tones.	All tones.	Rich warm grape or plum and pink, lavender or orchid.
Red	All tones.	Greyed tones and those without tint of yellow.	All tones except those with yellow tint.	All tones.	Wine tones.	Wine and dark tones rather than light.	Wine.
Yellow	Yes, except extremely light or excessively brilliant.	No.	All tones tangerine and henna.	All tones.	Some tones of henna, tangerine and orange	All tones.	No.

							Rose.
	All tones.	Rose rather than real pinks.	All tones.	All tones.	Rose tones best.	All tones.	
Pink							
Black	Yes, with or without white or colors.	Can be worn with white about face.	Yes.	Yes.	Yes, with white at neck.	Yes.	Yes, if with cream white about the face.
White	Yes, cream and ivory, better than blue white and green white.	Cream and ivory with black and dark colors above blue white rather than green white.	All tones.	All tones.	Cream and ivory best.	All tones if hair is clear and brilliant.	Cream and ivory.
Grey	The lighter tones preferable.	The lighter tones especially those with a pink tint.	All tones.	All tones.	Medium tones preferably with white at neck.	All tones and especially when combined with color.	With tint of rose.

†If eyes are pale all colors used should be low in tone, that is, not brilliant.

*If complexion is florid avoid tones too brilliant, and provide for white near the face.

The Importance of the Corset

Ever since 1547, when Catherine of Medici introduced the corset into the French Court, it has been regarded by European women in society as an essential of correct dressing. Even as far back as that, Paris was the centre of fashion, and what the Queen of France favoured was necessarily destined to be adopted by all people in all countries aspiring to social importance. The corset of the sixteenth century, however, was a very different garment to that worn by the woman of to-day.

Catherine of Medici's waist measured thirteen inches. Sixteen inches was the utmost permitted to ladies of the court. Their corsets were made of bands of steel riveted together. In course of time fabric corsets, reinforced with steel or whale-bone stays, replaced the old all-metal instrument of torture, but even these, until late years, were unhygienic. The ideal of the small waist has died hard, and it is only within the last twenty years that comfort and health have been considered important by the designers and manufacturers. The medical profession used to rail at the unnatural compression of organs which was general when practically all civilised women in Europe, America and Australia followed the fashion, having for its ideal smallness of waist measurement rather than the symmetry and grace of normally developed and healthy womanhood.

The fit and hang of your gown, and your figure's grace and harmony of line depend in a large measure upon your corset. It is better to wear a simple, inexpensive dress over a good corset than the most costly gown over an indifferent one.

French women, noted throughout the world for their correctness in dress, spend as much as they can afford in having a really suitable and well-fitting corset. They give much thought to the choice of it, look after it with great care, and always put it on and take it off the right way. By this means they make it last a long time, keeping its shape and enhancing the fit and style of their gowns to the last.

In choosing your corset, make sure that you get the model that has been designed for your type of figure, and buy a good one. Slim women may occasionally economise by buying cheap corsets, but stout women must never do it.

The first word of warning concerns new dresses. Do not wear one corset when being fitted for a new frock and another when you wear it; to do so is quite wrong. You cannot expect the dress to look alright over a different corset, especially if the two models are cut on different lines.

Now-a-days tightness is not admired. Get your corsets comfortably loose in the waist and above it. They may be firmly laced below the waist if desired, especially if there is a tendency to heaviness around the hips and abdomen. Slender women should get lightly-boned corsets, and, if thin on the hip select free hip models, which have one stay over the hip-bone. If unable to buy a free-hip model, the thin women should make little wadding pads and sew them to the under side of the corset where the stays press. They require two pairs of suspenders.

The Modern Corset—Graceful, Comfortable, and Hygienic.

Stout women require close-boned models and skirts to their corsets which are long at the sides and back, with two or three pairs of suspenders. The third pair helps to hold the skirt well down over the flesh at the back of the hips. Whilst the corset skirt should be long, the bones need not be long below the waist, except at the side. The front especially should be short, as it is both uncomfortable and unsightly, when sitting, to have the front of the corset pushed up through the bone being too long. This particularly applies to the short-waisted, whether slim or stout. This is, of course, general advice, which may be applied according to your particular style.

Now as to yourself: Find the particular make and model which gives your figure the most desirable lines. Learn the number when the corset is new—later it may be obliterated—and make a note of it. Afterwards, having found your own particular model, stick to it and ask for it by number. If the shop tells you that they are out of that particular one, suggesting a substitute, just a little higher in price, saying that it is the same cut, but better, refuse to take it, unless you prove it to be the same and do not mind paying extra. If you will not take a substitute, they will usually get your model for you from the warehouse rather than lose a sale; if not, go to another shop stocking that model, or write to the warehouse and ask them to supply you and credit the shop where you would buy the corset.

Figures may be classed into three main groups—slender, average and stout. These three again into tall and short, and the stout still further into full above and full below the waistline. All corset manufacturers will cater for these specified types. Some of them will go still further by dividing the long or short backed, erect, stooping, etc. However, you need not trouble to look for these variations. If you go to a good corset fitter, she will show you suitable models for you to try on and, if you have not already found the one which is just right, by all means let her try on one pair after another till you find it.

THE SHORT SLENDER WOMAN requires a corset which will accentuate her slim grace and suppleness, but will tend to lengthen her lines. This is a matter of the right cut. It should be moderately short and light in weight.

THE TALL SLENDER WOMAN must also have her corsets lightly boned, but longer than her short sister. Particularly see that they are long enough at the sides to ensure an unbroken line from waist to hip.

THE SHORT-WAISTED WOMAN, WHETHER SLENDER, AVERAGE OR STOUT, should seek a corset designed to make her lines appear longer. It should be worn loosely and well pulled down. Three pairs of suspenders will be a help in this. The front should be short, particularly below the waist.

THE WOMAN OF MEDIUM OR AVERAGE FIGURE, approximately nearest to the ideal, is fortunate in being able to choose from a wide range of models. She should nevertheless exercise no less care in getting that which best enhances her good points, aiming at the suggestion of youthful slimness if her lines are straight, or trim roundness if her curves are more pronounced.

THE SHORT STOUT WOMAN must be most careful to get her corsets comfortable as well as becoming. She cannot get any comfort out of corsets too long, especially in the front. First of all they must be well and firmly-boned of strong material. She must have them loosely-laced at the waist and above and well pulled down, then drawn in tightly around the hips. A well-fitting brassiere is also essential—one with an elastic section is especially suitable.

If she has any difficulty in getting her corset right in every particular, she had better have a pair altered to fit her. It can easily be made shorter in the front or otherwise made to suit.

The most primitive mind can absorb by example.
The world you see is often the image of your heart.
Deepen the happiness of as many hearts as you can.
Whenever we are sincerely pleased we are nourished.

THE TALL STOUT WOMAN must also take care in her choice of her corset, but is really easier to fit than when she is short and stout. Hers must be longer in every way, of strong material, and very heavily-boned to retain its shape and control her lines. The skirts must be quite long, and a second piece laced over the abdomen is also sometimes useful.

A brassiere must be worn.

THE FIGURE HEAVY BELOW THE WAIST is most difficult of all to fit. Its owner should consult a corset fitter about her corset and, if necessary, have a pair either made to order or reinforced to suit her. Double fronts below the waist or an extra lacing here are useful, and several pairs of suspenders will help to control the extra fulness.

A Well-fitting Brassiere helps to give smooth, trim lines to the fleshy woman.

THE FULL-BUSTED FIGURE is best in a corset that is very loose, at and above the waist, so that there is room for the extra flesh to fall inside it. A well-fitting brassiere, with elastic filets let in and well laced up, helps to flatten the bust and keeps a smooth line at the top of the corset, both front and back.

HOW TO KEEP YOUR CORSETS IN GOOD CONDITION AND MAKE THEM WEAR A LONG TIME.

If you wear corsets at all wear them always. Keep two or three pairs at least in wear—quite old ones for housework, gardening, or vacation wear; your second best for afternoon wear at home; and your newest pair for dress occasions.

For dancing, tennis and other games many women, particularly the slender, wear a girdle, which is very lightly boned and little more than a suspender belt. This is quite a good idea and most suitable for sports model clothes.

Should your corsets become damp with perspiration, hang them in the air to dry and freshen before putting them away or wearing them again. Occasionally they should be washed, or, if of the very expensive kind, they may be dry-cleaned. Corsets of ordinary material wash very well, and practically all of them nowadays are rustless. Let them first lie in clean lukewarm, not hot, water for about ten minutes. Rinse them up and down in this and drain it off, spread them on a clean table and scrub all over on both sides with a strong brush dipped constantly in hot soapsuds from a good white cleansing soap. Rinse several

Modern Corset for the Woman with full hips.

times in lukewarm water, pull into shape and peg on line in the sun and wind to dry. When nearly dry, put them on, so as to stretch them into shape, then hang out again.

Do not boil corsets, as it ruins the elastic in the suspenders or other parts. Should they be discolored, you may dye them any pale color with one of the many good cold-water dyes on the market. Do this after washing.

Corset laces should be washed whenever they look soiled.

Many women pay a good price for their corsets, but do not get the good appearance out of them that they should, chiefly because they do not put them on and take them off the right way. They lace them up all the way and leave them so, putting them on and off with the lacing fastened. This is quite wrong. The laces should be untied and loosened before putting on and drawn in and adjusted on the figure—hips first, bust next, waist last. If you do not know how to do this just right, get the corset saleswoman to do it the first time and follow her example afterwards.

Before taking them off again, loosen them till they nearly fall off and unhook the fronts whilst they are in this condition. Only in this way can you preserve their shape and hope to get the best results on your figure.

When the fog is too thick to see, you can always listen.

* * *

The surest sign of nobility of character is to be without envy.

* * *

The friction of life can be reduced by the magic of orderliness.

* * *

The most learned individuals sometimes have the least common sense.

* * *

Books mostly record man's long struggle to understand himself and his world.

Dainty Specials in Underwear

A PRETTY SLEEVELESS NIGHTDRESS FOR HOT WEATHER.

The nightie illustrated below will take about three yards of 36-inch material, or twice your length from shoulder to hem. For it, use your magyar nightdress pattern, and cut a fresh pattern as shown in the diagram, cutting a diagonal line from the arm-hole to a point high up on your dress form and see that the shoulder. Try this against the openings front and back are right; also mark on it a high waist line.

Cut out your nightdress from nainsook, crepe-de-chene, fuji silk, voile, etc.

Cut front and back alike, with the fold of the material to the middle of the pattern.

Join the sections with a felled seam. Finish the edges of the body either with a crossway facing, beading and edging whipped along the edges, scalloped buttonholing, or a crocheted edging into hemstitching.

Stitch a casing of the material about an inch wide on the under side along the high waist line or make eight or twelve buttonholes perpendicularly along this line to carry a pretty colored ribbon

A Charming Night-gown.

— about two yards, slightly narrower than the casing. Join the back and front shoulder points and tack a bow made from about half a yard each of the same ribbon. Turn up the bottom the right length with an inch hem.

If desired, spray of flowers in white or the same color as the material or a contrasting color may be embroidered in the points, and add very much to the beauty of the garment.

A WINTER NIGHT GOWN WITH SET-IN SLEEVES.

Make this of flannelette, wincey, nun's-veiling, flannel, or wool, or wool and cotton stocknette. The facing at the neck, front opening and cuffs make the trimming, and may be of a contrasting color or decorative material which will wash and wear well. The closing should be either in pearl buttons and button-holes, or by frogs made of braid of a harmonising color.

For a woman of average height the nightgown should take about four yards of 36-inch material for the nightdress itself, with half a yard of trimming material. Because of the diagonal closing, right and left fronts must be cut separately.

After cutting out the nightdress join the front and back breadths at the shoulder seams with a felled seam; then lay them on a piece of paper and cut out the neck and right front by it. Follow the outline of the edge, making a shaped border two inches round the neck and down the right front. Cut straight cuffs from a piece of material five inches wide and large enough for the hands to slip through. Pin and tack the facing with its right side to the wrong side of the nightdress, leaving about two inches loose at the bottom of the opening. Stitch strongly in the machine and turn over to the right side. Turn the edge of the facing under; pin and tack in position so that it lies nice and flat.

Make and stitch the pocket to the right front.

If the left front has a selvedge, it will not need to be hemmed or faced, but if it has a raw edge it must be finished in one of these two ways. Let a facing extend far enough to provide a double piece of material for sewing the buttons on. If a hem or a selvedge is used, run a piece of tape on the under side for carrying these, otherwise the material will tear with the strain of the button threads.

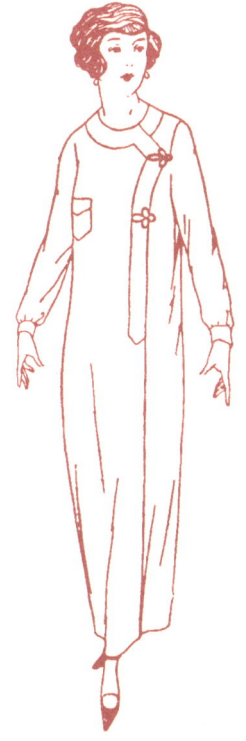

Stitch the facing round the front and sides; join the two fronts together with a felled seam. Tack the end of the facing over the top of the join and stitch neatly to join up with the stitching already on the facing.

Join backs and fronts together with a felled seam.

Join up the sleeve seams in the same way, and gather the bottom of the sleeves into the cuff-bands. Run a thread at the top of the sleeves and insert into the armholes, with their seams corresponding with the side-seams and corresponding notches matching. Either fell the sleeves in or stitch in and bind the raw edges with a crossway piece of the material.

Turn up the bottom of the nightgown with an inch hem.

Night-gown for Cold Weather.

TRY THIS CHARMING NEGLIGEE.

If you want to make something especially attractive for a bride or an honoured girl friend, make her this out of a square of some dainty fabric 36 or 40 inches wide. Crepe-de-chene, georgette, chiffon, ninon, silk voile, even cotton voile or cotton georgette, will make a very dainty affair, which will be welcome in any trousseau. Two layers of georgette in harmonising colors or shadow lace over chiffon, ninon or georgette would be charming. Two tassels, preferably of silk, otherwise of beads or a couple of bunches of wadding-stuffed bobs on twisted silk hanging threads will be necessary at the lower corners.

Try the pattern out in paper or cheap lining first. Fold it across the middle both ways to get the centre, and mark this point with a pin; spread it on a table and pin it down with drawing-pins. From the centre draw a circle, either with a compass or a pencil on a piece of cotton with a pin held in the centre of the circle, with a diameter of eight inches—that is, the circumference will be four inches from the centre. Draw the four sections of the neck opening the fold, taking care that they are all alike and correctly placed. Cut out the circle. Try over your head to see if it will pass comfortably. If necessary draw a line slightly outside this, but be careful not to make it too big in the opening, or it will slip over your shoulders when you put it on.

Solid material must be laid under the pattern; transparent material over the pattern. Pin it down with drawing-pins. Run a tacking thread around the neck line in the pattern before cutting. If you wish to hem it cut three-eighths of an inch inside the line and turn over a tiny hem. If you wish it hemstitched, do not cut the circle out until comes back from the hemstitcher's.

You may bind the neck if you prefer with a $\frac{3}{4}$-inch bias strip, in which case you will cut out the circle at the neckline.

The four sides may be hemmed, hemstitched or bound, as preferred. A Picot edge, made by cutting through a row of hemstitching, is a very pretty finish.

After cutting off all threads, sew on the tassels, and the negligee is finished.

Where double georgette or lace over georgette or chiffon is used, hem both squares independently at the four edges. Lay one over the other on the table, turn in a tiny edge of each neck opening to face one another,

A Charming Negligee.

and baste together at the neck with small stitches; bind the neck edge with a narrow bias strip of the underneath material. Catch the lower corners together with the tassels as with the single material. Do not join the two squares together anywhere else.

You cannot get the sweetness out of life by flinging the usefulness of it away.

* * *

No matter who says the word so long as it's the right one.

* * *

Always bow to Joy when you meet her on the streets of Life.

A Useful Kimono for Travelling

For this you will need three-and-a-half yards of 36 or 40-inch silk, such as shantung, crepe-de-chene, crepe meteor, morocaine, mousseline, etc., of one color, and a half-yard of a contrasting color for collar, cuffs and pocket. Of 30-inch silk, such as fuji silk, you will want four and three-quarters of the former for the length, and three-quarters of the latter.

The collar is cut double, and may be interlined with a soft cotton material, if desired.

The cuffs are really the wide lower half of the sleeves, made from sixteen inches wide and twelve inches deep. Cut out the half-yard of material this way:—

If you cannot get a pattern for the Kimono, you can cut it out like this:—

To get the pattern of the roll collar, join the shoulder seams of the fronts and backs with a French seam; then fold the back down the middle, and the fronts together. Place the back fold at the straight edge of a piece of paper large enough to extend to the front waistline. Pin the kimono down on the paper flat and cut along the neckline and down the front to the waistline. Lift off the kimono and draw half the collar, as shown in the diagram, beginning at nothing at the waistline and widening in a curve to about three inches in the middle of the back.

Join the top side of the collar to the neck of the kimono and

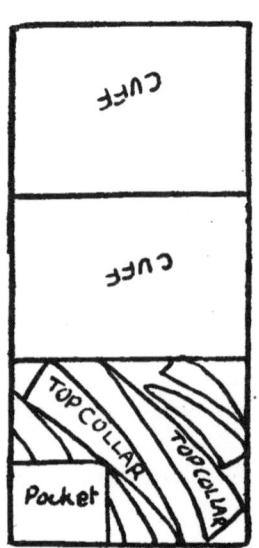

Diagram of Cuffs, Pocket, and Collar.

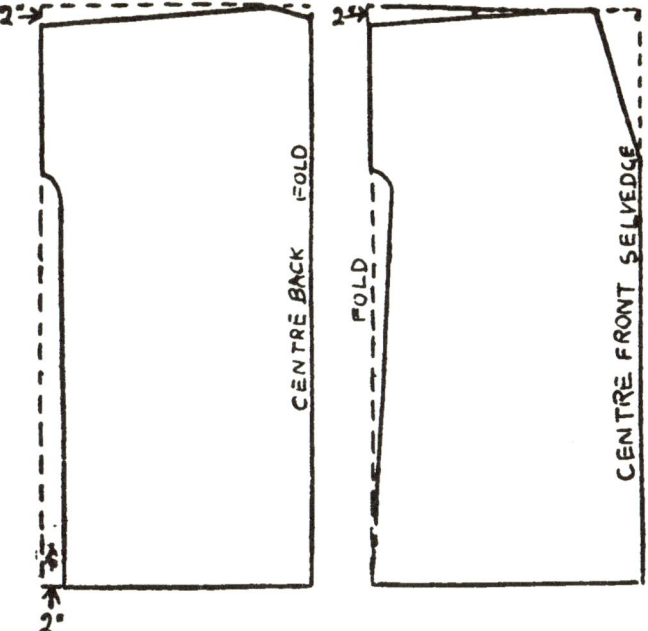

Diagram of Half Back and Half Front.

fell the under-side over the raw edges. Stitch the pocket to the right front and face the lower parts of the right and left front with the strips cut from the lower parts of the back, if cut from 40-inch material. If from 36-inch material, turn back the selvedge in a small hem and face the places where the button and button-hole are to be with circles of the material cut from the piece which comes out of the front neck opening.

Attach the top edges of the cuffs to the arm-holes. Join the fronts and backs at the underarm seams with a French seam from cuff to hem. Turn the cuffs under and fell the lower edges over the raw edges at the join at the arm-holes.

Turn up the bottom hem. Make a bound button-hole from the trimming material on the right front and sew a large button on the left front to correspond.

RIBBON GARTERS ARE DELIGHTFUL.

These are really quite inexpensive to make, and yet very expensive to buy. At sale time many of the shops offer ribbons at a good reduction. That is the time to buy the materials. Get silk elastic about half-an-inch wide. It usually takes about a yard and a quarter for a pair.

Use two strands of ribbon for each garter, half as long again as the elastic is to be when joined. The two strands are pretty when of two colors—orange and lemon, royal blue and jade, black and red, baby blue and flesh, pink and mauve, white and primrose, white and black, or any other combination desired.

The elastic may be joined and the ribbons sewn together over it, but the easiest method is to run both edges of the ribbon together and then to thread the elastic through them; join the elastic, then neatly and invisibly slip-stitch together the ends of the ribbon on either side of it.

A Useful Kimono.

Trim the garters at the joins with ribbon bows, flowers or fruit, or with rosettes of lace or ribbon. The ribbon fruit may contain sachet powder in with the wadding, or tiny satin sachet bags in matching color may be stitched into the loops of the bows or pinned with a little gilt safety-pin to the under side of the garters. A frill of lace may be gathered into the top edge of the ribbon to match a boudoir cap or negligee, also so trimmed.

A pretty gift to a bride is a pair of white and pale blue ribbon garters, with a spray of orange blossom for trimming.

CAMISOLE IDEAS.

Nowadays we need many and various camisoles. Under white and pale colored blouses and jumpers, pastel-tinted crepe-de-chene or washing satin are favoured. Dark colored outer garments with any transparency about them demand camisoles to match. Hand-knitted or crocheted jumpers, particularly require a pretty, solid, matching slip.

One yard of 40-inch material makes three camisoles to wear under blouses or two for wearing under jumpers. Join up the selvedges and turn under a small hem at the top and a wider hem at the bottom. The blouse camisole has an elastic threaded through the bottom hem, but the jumper camisole hangs straight over the skirt. Matching ribbon shoulder straps are attached to the tops, five inches apart at the back and seven inches apart in the front. They are usually 14 to 16 inches long, but the length is best determined by trying them on, as they are equally uncomfortable if they strain through tightness or fall over the shoulders through being too long. Unless the ribbon washes well, attach it with small gilt safety-pins, hidden under bows, instead of sewing it in position.

There are various ways of trimming these dainty camisoles: Wreaths of French knots or eyelet embroidery in self or contrasting colors, flat bows or narrow ribbon, tinsel thread couched in a trailing pattern, wee rosettes of lace or georgette or inset lace motifs are all pretty. A narrow piece of tucked georgette along the top or a row of hemstitching makes a good finish.

RIBBON AND RIBBON-TRIMMED CAMISOLES.

Camisoles made entirely of ribbon plain and chene, alternate vertical bands fagotted together, are very pretty. Then again, ribbon may alternate with filet, guipure or val lace insertion in the same manner, used horizontally. A yard and a quarter of wide ribbon joined under one arm, with a band of lace above it, is quite a favorite, and needs no other trimming except, perhaps, little bows or rosettes where the shoulder-straps are attached.

All over lace makes a satisfactory fancy camisole and, untrimmed or merely bound with a bias strip of crepe-de-chene, washes well. It may be trimmed, however, with a gathered binding of ribbon at the top, and bebe ribbon gathered at one edge may be used to outline some of the motifs in the lace pattern. Tinsel ribbon in large bows may be stitched flat on each side of the front.

Color may be introduced to show through the tinsel if desired.

PRETTY BLOOMERS.

A special pair of dainty bloomers, that also give extra warmth round the knees, are made from milanese, silk jersey, or crepe-de-chene by cutting them about five inches longer in the leg than usual. Run two light elastics in a casing, having a tuck half an inch wide top and bottom.

A pocket about four inches wide, stitched a little below the hip on the right front, is also a valuable feature where the outer garments are pocketless.

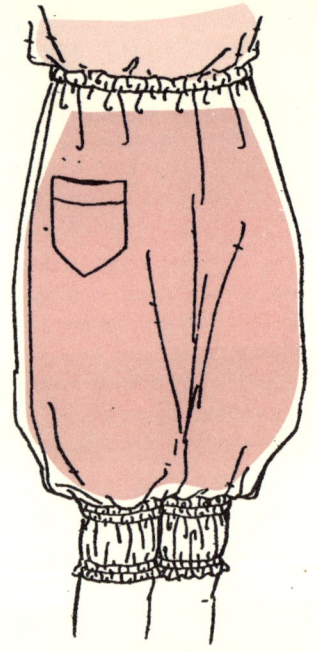

A Pair of Pretty Bloomers.

A PRACTICAL BRASSIERE.

A Brassiere which is especially useful for slight and average women, it is strong, easily laundered, and easy and inexpensive to make. Cut it from calico, cotton crepe, allover embroidery, or double mosquito net. The front is almost a straight strip, slightly curving up in the middle, and should be from six to nine inches deep, according to the size of the wearer; the back is quite straight, from four to six inches deep. It closes at the centre back, and the front is gathered to the back under the arm. After taking the bust measure rather tightly, allow the front breadth to be about two inches longer than the back, and allow half-an-inch on each side of the back for overlap as well as turnings.

A DAINTY APRON.

Look through your piece drawer and see if you have not got the materials for making one of these aprons. The pieces over from making a dress or blouse of muslin, cotton voile, lawn, crepe or linen would find a practical and acceptable application if devoted to this purpose. One piece about eighteen inches wide, or three pieces about six inches wide are required, and as long as desired or as the material cut—say twenty-one inches to the tip of the scallops. Join the strips, either with insertion or beading, fagoting or piping according to the material and what trimming you have on hand. Trim the edge with a row of insertion and edging, edging only, insertion and a frill, a frill only, or bind it with a bias strip. The apron illustrated is a particularly charming thing of dotted Swiss muslin with fine val. insertion and edging. A primrose satin ribbon trims the top and furnishes strings, whilst bows of this also appear at the right front waistline and on the pocket, where the dainty Miss may keep her hankie.

A Dainty Apron.

SPONGING AND SHRINKING MATERIAL.

It is very disappointing to find your garments grow smaller or lose their shape with wear. To prevent this, all woollen and linen materials, unless previously shrunk before purchasing, and many cotton goods, should be shrunk before making up. Sometimes the shop selling them will do this for an extra charge, or the local tailor may be willing to do it.

Either cut off the edge of the selvedge or snip it at close intervals. Cotton or linen materials should be immersed in cold water for about twenty minutes. Leave them in their original folds, but move them about from time to time to see that the water gets right through them. Do not wring, but press the water out with the hands, then hang on the line, taking care that the edges are not pulled out of shape. If colored, be sure to hang in a shady spot or the sun will fade them.

The shrinking of woollens requires time, care, patience, and a hot, heavy iron, as well as a small sheet or large cotton cloth. Do not use a sheet you want to have white again for the beds, as it is liable to become badly discolored, perhaps, scorched, in the process.

Lay the material singly face downwards on a padded table. Wring out the sheet from cold water and place over it and press every portion of it with the hot iron till all the moisture is drawn out. Do not rub; press and lift the iron all the time. Woollen pile fabrics should not be shrunk except by an expert.

CORRECT PRESSING.

One of the reasons why tailored garments look so well is because they are always so beautifully pressed. The best-made woollen coat or dress can never look right unless it is well and truly pressed at every stage.

Lay the material face down on the ironing board with a dry ironing sheet over it. Dampen the place to be pressed with a wet sponge. Place the iron on this spot, but do not move it along. Keep it there till it is perfectly dry. Lift the iron and move it to the adjoining spot its length away, lift again, and so on. Do not ever let the iron stay long enough on one spot to mark the material.

If, in pressing, you have made the material shiny, lay it on the ironing-board with the shiny spots up. Lay a damp cloth over them and hold the iron there long enough for them to become well steamed. Remove iron and cloth quickly and brush the steam into the material.

For silks and satins, do not use moisture, but place a sheet of clean white tissue paper over the material, and use an iron not hot enough to scorch. Scorching happens very easily with silk or satin.

For velvets, turn and iron upside down, and draw the material over it, wrong side to the iron.

Table of Materials

Giving name, width and general description to aid in identification for the purchasing and proper use of materials.

One of the fundamentals of correct dressing is the proper application of material to the design, the proper selection of material for the garments of different character.

Name.	Width—Inches.	Description.
Batiste	36 & 40	A soft finish cotton material used in the less expensive qualities for all sorts of lingeries, babies' dresses and underwear. The finer qualities are used for blouses, summer dresses for women and children. Comes in white and pale solid colors, also in figured designs.
Bedford Cord	36	Light-weight wool fabric with a round cord in the weave. Used for babies' and children's coats principally.
Bengaline	36	A soft silk with round medium heavy cord used for covering and trimming hats, for dresses and wraps.
Bolivia Cloth	54	A soft, thick, light-weight cloth of wool with sometimes a small admixture of silk used for winter coats and wraps.
Burlap	36	Roughly woven cotton material used for draperies and upholstery.
Calico	27 to 36	White or grey (unbleached), dressed or undressed, ranging from coarse, loosely woven and low priced to firmly and finely woven at three times the price of the former. Used for underwear, shirts and aprons. Treated with rubber becomes waterproof sheeting.

Name.	Width—Inches.	Description.
Cambric	27 to 36	Fine white or colored cotton material. Used for petticoats, dresses, lingerie, babies' clothes and children's underwear.
Canton crepe	36 to 40	Heavy silk of crepy texture and satiny finish, used for dresses, blouses, summer wraps and capes.
Canvas	18 to 36	Cotton or linen fabric stiffened with glue. Used for stiffening men's coat collars and revers principally, or for facings where a little body is necessary.
Challis	28 to 32	Comes in both cotton and wool. The cotton challis is used for negligees and quilt covering. Wool challis is used for ladies' and children's dresses, and for elaborate negligees. Generally shows a cream ground with colored figures or floral designs. French challis also comes with colored ground.
Chambray	27-32	Cotton fabric of plain weave in light weight. Colored warp with white filling. Generally in solid colors. Used for morning and house dresses, for aprons, children's dresses, boys' blouses, and little boys' washing suits.
Charmeuse	36-40	A soft finish satin with wool back. very soft and lustrous. Used for handsome dresses, and wraps.
Cheviot	44-50-54	Wool material with rough weave, sometimes has a rib woven in. Comes in plain colors, as well as with threads of contrasting color woven in. Used for coats, heavy suits, men's and boys' clothes.

Name.	Width—Inches.	Description.
Chiffon	39-40	A thin sheer silk material in solid colors as well as all sorts of printed designs. Used for afternoon and evening dresses, wedding gowns, scarfs, hats, trimmings and negligees.
Corduroy	27-32-36	A ribbed fabric with a close pile. The more expensive qualities have cotton warp and silk pile. Comes in white and colors. White is used for babies' coats and sports skirts. The colored is used for suits and coats, and bath robes. In grey or brown for boys' knock-about suits. Also for infants' carriage covers.
Cotton crepe	24 to 40	A crinkled fabric light in weight. Comes in plain solid colors and figured and floral effects. Used for negligees, pyjamas, lingerie, dresses and sometimes blouses. Also good for little girls' bloomer dresses.
Covert cloth	44-54	Closely woven smooth finish wool material used for coats, suits, and riding habits.
Cravenette cloth	54	A wool material treated by a special process so that it is practically waterproof. Used principally for rain coats and knock-about skirts.
Crepe-de-Chene	36-40	Finely crinkled soft lightweight silk. Used for lingerie, negligees, dresses and blouses.
Cretonne	27-36-54	Cotton cloth slightly heavy in weight, generally in figured and floral effects. Used for curtains, draperies and upholstery, sport dresses, bungalow aprons, little girls' frocks, millinery, household utility bags, luncheon sets.

Name.	Width—Inches.	Description.
Denim	27-36	Heavy durable cotton material in uneven twilled weave. Used for overalls, furniture covering and upholstery.
Dimity	32-36	Fine cotton fabric corded or cross-barred in white and delicate colors—frequently in floral designs. Suitable for summer frocks for ladies and children, and for negligees, lingerie, curtains, bureau and dresser scarfs.
Drill	32-36	Coarse cotton material with twill weave. Used for men's trousers, middy blouses, separate summer skirts, boys' washing suits and childrn's dresses.
Duck	27 to 36	Heavy-weight twilled cotton fabric. Used for sports skirts, middy blouses, men's outing trousers, tents.
Duvetyn	36-54	A lovely soft material. In the 36 inch width, the wool is mixed with silk forming a light-weight material used for winter dressy frocks and blouses. The 54 inch has the same lovely finish but is wool and is heavier in weight. Used for handsome wraps, coats and suits.
Faille	36-40	Ribbed weave soft silk. Used for handsome dresses, and for ladies' and children's dressy coats, infants' bonnets and millinery.
Flannelette	27-30-36	Cotton fabric with slight woolly looking nap. Used for pyjamas, kimonos, winter nightgowns and petticoats.

Name.	Width—Inches.	Description
Foulard	36-40	Figured soft silk with slight twill. Used for ladies' dresses, and occasionally for lining coats and jackets.
Gabardine	44-50-54	Wool fabric with rather hard worsted weave and fine twill. Used for ladies' dresses, suits, and coats. Children's coats.
Galatea	27-32-36	Heavy firm cotton material in solid colors and stripes. Used for outing blouses and dresses—boys' wash suits, little girls' sailor dresses.
Georgette crepe	39-40	A lovely sheer silk crepe with very fine crepy finish. Comes in plain colors and in a wide variety of figured and floral designs. Used for ladies' and girls' dresses, blouses, negligees, lingerie and hats.
Gingham	27-32-36	Cotton material dyed in the yarn before weaving. A big variety of checks and plaids formed from combinations of warp and woof. Comes also in plain solid colors. Used for dresses and aprons.
Homespun	54	Soft wool loosely woven fabric sometimes in solid color, sometimes with woven threads of contrasting color. Used for ladies' suits, utility coats, men's and boys' suits, and light-weight top coats.
Lawn	36	Semisheer cotton fabric unfilled, filled with starch or sizing. Comes in solid colors as well as a variety of printed designs. Used for ladies', misses and chidren's dresses, and for negligees.

Name.	Width—Inches.	Description
Linen	27 to 45	Woven from flax in medium and light-weight and used for dresses, suits, blouses, summer motor coats, separate summer skirts, middy blouses, boys' summer suits and children's dresses, underwear, handkerchiefs, napery, etc.
Longcloth	36-40	A soft finish white cotton fabric, closely woven. Used for lingerie, infants' dresses, slips, and petticoats, and children's underwear.
Lonsdale cambric	36	Light-weight white cotton fabric with slight stiffening. Used for ladies' and children's underwear.
Madras	27-32	Firmly woven cotton material, sometimes all white, plain or with a cord at intervals, or white fround with a colored stripe, Used for men's pyjamas and shirts, and boys' blouses. Also ladies' shirt-waists.
Mull	27-32-36	Soft, silky, semisheer fabric made of cotton or silk. Used for dresses, princess foundation slips, summer blouses and sometimes for lining thin dresses. Infants' and children's bonnets and hats.
Muslin	36 to 108	Light-weight cotton frabic, used for under-wear, dresses, blouses, millinery, babies clothing, handkerchiefs, curtains, etc.
Mohair	36-40-44	Glossy rather stiff material woven from Angora wool generally mixed with cotton. Because of its finish, is good for motor coats and for bathing suits as it sheds dust and water.

Name.	Width—Inches.	Description
Moire	36-40	Silk with watered effect, obtained by pressing between rollers.
Nainsook	36-40-45	Light-weight soft finish white cotton fabric used for lingerie and for infants' clothes.
Net	18 to 72	Sheer diaphanous weave fabric—the cheaper quality in cotton, the more expensive woven of silk. Used for evening dresses, draperies and flounces over satin or silk, for scarfs, hats and hat trimming. The coarser cotton weave is sometimes called bobbinet and is used for curtains, bed spreads, etc.
Organdie	40-45	Fine weave sheer cotton fabric, stiffened. In white, delicate color and fancy weaves. Used for ladies', misses, and children's dresses. Summer millinery.
Percale	36	Plain weave firm cotton material, generally in printed designs, used for simple morning and house-dresses, shirts, pyjamas, boys' washing suits, rompers and aprons.
Percaline	36-40	Firm, closely woven cotton fabric, with glazed finish. Used principally for lining.
Pique	27-32-40	A firm cotton fabric with fine or heavy lengthwise cord. Used for vests, cravats, boys' washing suits, separate summer skirts, and as trimming on dresses, and for collars and cuffs on jackets.
Point d'esprit	40 to 72	Fine sheer net with a small dot. Used for blouses, evening wear and for elaborate lingerie dresses.

Name.	Width—Inches.	Description
Pongee	27-32	Soft unbleached wash silk woven in China—the product of wild silk-worms that feed on oak leaves. Used for dresses, underwear, blouses and negligees. Usually in natural color but sometimes dyed.
Poplin	27-32-44	Fine corded weave in cotton, silk, silk and wool, and all wool. Cotton poplin is used for summer dresses, skirts and blouses, the silk and wool poplins are used for afternoon frocks, children's and infants' coats.
Poiret twill	44-54	Firm closely woven wool fabric with a delicate twill. Used for tailored dresses, suits, and light-weight coats.
Prunella cloth	44-54	Strongly woven woollen fabric with slight diagonal cord, formerly used for clergymen's gowns. Now used for tailored dresses and separate skirts. Comes in solid colors, plaids and stripes.
Print	27-32	Strong cotton fabric with printed figures. Used in less expensive quality for house-dresses, negligees, aprons, children's rompers and play dresses. The higher-priced prints make good-looking summer dresses for ladies and children.
Rep	32 to 54	Strong twilled material with decided cord in weave. Comes in cotton and wool. Used for boys' washing suits, children's dresses, collars, and cuffs, separate skirts, draperies and furniture covering.

Name.	Width—Inches.	Description
Sateen	32-36	Close, firmly woven cotton material with glossy finish resembling satin in plain colors and floral, and other patterns. Used for lining, children's dresses, and ladies' summer dresses.
Satin	18 to 40	A silk fabric of thick close texture, with lustrous face and dull back, the glossy surface being attained by finishing between hot rollers.
Serge	44 to 54	Wool fabric of hard twisted worsted with woven twill. Generally in solid colors. Used for ladies' and misses' tailored dresses, suits, coats and separate skirts, children's coats and dresses, boys' and men's suits.
Shepherd check	44-48	Soft wool fabric principally in small black and white checks. Used for separate skirts, suits, girls' dresses and coats.
Soisette	36	Soft twilled cotton fabric used for negligees, shirts, pyjamas and boys' blouses. Also used for ladies' and misses' tailored blouses.
Swiss	32 to 45	Sheer thin muslin with stiff finish, comes in solid colors, dots, stripes and figures. Used for dresses, fancy aprons and curtains.
Taffeta	36-40	Fine glossy untwilled silk sometimes given body by artificial stiffening. Used for dresses, summer suits, coat and jacket linings, hats, and wraps.
Tricolet	36	Knitted fabric of artificial silk with high lustre. Used for blouses and dresses.

Name.	Width—Inches.	Description.
Tricotine	44 to 54	Heavy twill wool fabric principally in solid colors. Used for dresses, suits and coats.
Tweed	54	Hard finish wool fabric usually with two or more colors in the yarn. Used for women's sports suits, separate skirts, utility top coats and men's suits.
Velvet	24-44	A thick closely woven silk fabric having on the right side a soft thick nap or pile. Used for trimming, for hats, and for winter dresses, suits and wraps.
Velveteen	27 to 36	Cotton velvet. Used for the same purposes as velvet, but less costly.
Voile	36-40	Hard twisted warp and wool threads woven in open mesh. Comes in all cotton, and silk and cotton. Used for dresses and blouses, curtains, negligees and summer underwear.
Whipcord	54	Woollen fabric made of hard twisted yarn. Shows a fine cord. Used for riding habits and occasionally suits and top coats.
Wool Jersey	54	Soft, knitted, wool fabric used for dresses, blouses and utility and sports suits and coats.

LIST OF ILLUSTRATIONS

Any illustrations not listed below appeared in the original edition of the publication.

Page 7	Advertisement for women's accessories, *The Myer Emporium Ltd*, Melbourne, catalogue, Winter 1926. Australian Collection
Page 10	'Brushes of Every Description', advertisement, *Furniture: The House for Good Values—W. & T. Rhodes Ltd*, Adelaide, catalogue, 1922. Australian Collection.
Page 16	Advertisements for baby's high chairs and for baby's pram, *Cribb and Foote*, catalogue, 1930s. Ephemera Collection
Page 21	Advertisement for assorted children's toys and accessories, *The Myer Emporium Ltd*, Melbourne, catalogue, Autumn/Winter 1926. Australian Collection
Page 24	Illustration from *The Myer Emporium Ltd*, Melbourne, catalogue, Spring/Christmas 1926. Australian Collection
Page 32	'Murdoch's Travelling Requisites', advertisement for luggage, *Murdoch's Autumn/Winter Catalogue*, 1922. Ephemera Collection
Pages 37	'Distinctive New Millinery' (detail), advertisement for women's accesories, *Advanced Style Direct from London to Brussels*, catalogue, 1916. Ephemera Collection
Pages 38, 43	Illustrations from *The Myer Emporium Ltd*, Melbourne, catalogue, Spring/Christmas, 1925. Australian Collection
Page 49	Advertisement for men's accessories, *The Myer Emporium Ltd*, Melbourne, catalogue, Spring/Christmas 1926. Australian Collection
Page 52	Advertisement for women's umbrellas, *The Myer Emporium Ltd*, Melbourne, catalogue, Spring/Christmas 1926. Australian Collection
Page 57	Illustration from *The Myer Emporium Ltd*, Melbourne, catalogue, Autumn/Winter 1927. Australian Collection
Page 64	Advertisement for LUX soap, *Fashion Carries On*, fashion parade booklet, The Myer Emporium Ltd, Melbourne, Autumn/Winter 1941. Ephemera Collection
Page 73	Advertisement for women's fur coats, *The Myer Emporium Ltd*, Melbourne, catalogue, Spring/Christmas 1926. Australian Collection
Page 75	Advertisement for assorted children's toys, *The Myer Emporium Ltd*, Melbourne, catalogue, Spring/Christmas 1926. Australian Collection
Page 76	'Distinctive New Millinery' (detail), advertisement for women's accesories, *Advanced Style Direct from London to Brussels*, catalogue, 1916. Ephemera Collection
Page 81	Advertisement for cologne (detail), *Bussell's*, catalogue, 1920s. Ephemera Collection

Page 84	Illustration from *Advanced Style Direct from London to Brussels*, catalogue, 1916. Ephemera Collection
Page 89	Advertisement for men's sporting equipment, *The Myer Emporium Ltd*, Melbourne, catalogue, Spring/Christmas 1926. Australian Collection
Page 90	'D&A "Non Rustable" No. 624' (detail), advertisement for women's corsets, *Advanced Style Direct from London to Brussels*, catalogue, 1916. Ephemera Collection
Page 94	Advertisement for a woman's manicure set (detail), *Advanced Style Direct from London to Brussels*, catalogue, 1916. Ephemera Collection
Page 95	Illustration from *The Mutual Store*, Melbourne, catalogue, 1930s. Ephemera Collection
Page 98	Advertisement for glassware, *Finney's Autumn/Winter Catalogue*, 1928. Ephemera Collection
Page 105	Advertisement for cutlery sets (detail), *The Myer Emporium Ltd*, Melbourne, catalogue, Spring/Christmas 1925. Australian Collection
Page 115	Advertisement for glassware (details), *Finney's Autumn/Winter Catalogue*, 1928. Ephemera Collection
Page 119	Advertisement for teapot, *Furniture: The House for Good Values—W. & T. Rhodes Ltd*, Adelaide, catalogue, 1922. Australian Collection
Page 121	Advertisements for stoves, *Furniture: The House for Good Values—W. & T. Rhodes Ltd*, Adelaide, catalogue, 1922. Australian Collection
Page 126	Advertisement for cutlery (detail), *The Myer Emporium Ltd*, Melbourne, catalogue, Winter 1926. Australian Collection
Page 128	Advertisement for confectionery (detail), *Cribb and Foote*, catalogue, 1930s. Ephemera Collection
Page 132	Advertisement for glassware (reversed detail), *Finney's Autumn/Winter Catalogue*, 1928. Ephemera Collection
Page 134	'Crystal Goblet Sets Reflecting Exquisite Taste', advertisement, *Cribb and Foote*, catalogue, 1930s. Ephemera Collection
Page 136	Advertisement for glassware (details), *Finney's Autumn/ Advertisement for cutlery (detail), The Myer Emporium Ltd, Melbourne, catalogue, Winter 1926. Australian Collection Winter Catalogue*, 1928. Ephemera Collection
Page 142	Advertisement for women's clothing (detail), *Finney's Autumn/Winter Catalogue*, 1928. Ephemera Collection
Page 146	'Ladies' Bags', advertisement, *Simpson's Catalogue of Leather Goods*, 1920s.
Page 177	Illustration from *The Myer Emporium Ltd*, Melbourne, catalogue, Spring/Christmas 1925. Australian Collection
Page 182	Illustration from *The Myer Emporium Ltd*, Melbourne, catalogue, Autumn/Winter 1927. Australian Collection